P9-DFU-152

JOHNSBURG PUBLIC LIBRARY

3 8164 00044 8201

Johnsburg Public Library
3000 West Johnsburg Road
Johnsburg, IL 60050
Phone: 815-344-0077

THE WHALE

Look for these and other books in the
Lucent Endangered Animals and Habitat series:

The Elephant
The Giant Panda
The Oceans
The Rhinoceros
The Shark
The Whale

Other related titles in the Lucent Overview series:

Acid Rain
Endangered Species
Energy Alternatives
Garbage
The Greenhouse Effect
Ocean Pollution
Oil Spills
Ozone
Pesticides
Population
Rainforests
Recycling
Vanishing Wetlands
Zoos

THE WHALE

BY ADAM WOOG

Endangered
Animals &
Habitats

Johnsburg Public Library
3000 West Johnsburg Road
Johnsburg, IL 60050
Phone: 815-344-0077

LUCENT BOOKS, INC.
SAN DIEGO, CALIFORNIA

LUCENT *Overview Series*

Library of Congress Cataloging-in-Publication Data

Woog, Adam, 1953–
    The Whale / by Adam Woog.
        p.   cm. — (Endangered animals & habitats)
(Lucent overview series)
    Includes bibliographical references (p.   ) and index.
    Summary: Presents an overview of various species of whale, how
they have become endangered, and what is being done to protect
them from extinction.
    ISBN 1-56006-460-9 (alk. paper)
    1. Whales—Juvenile literature.   2. Endangered species—
Juvenile literature.   [1. Whales.   2. Endangered species.]
I. Title.   II. Series.   III. Series: Lucent overview series.
QL737.C42W66   1998
599.5—dc21   97-21349
                                                             CIP
                                                             AC

No part of this book may be reproduced or used in any form or by any means, electrical,
mechanical, or otherwise, including, but not limited to, photocopy, recording, or any information storage and retrieval system, without prior written permission from the publisher.

Copyright © 1998 by Lucent Books, Inc.
P.O. Box 289011, San Diego, CA 92198-9011
Printed in the U.S.A.

Contents

Introduction

WHALES ARE SOME of the most amazing creatures in the world. For thousands of years, people have been enthralled by their enormous size, majestic power, and massive grace. The fact that until very recently humans knew little about whales' mysterious lives only added to the intrigue. "The whale is the most astonishing animal the earth has ever known," the undersea explorer Jacques-Yves Cousteau has written. "It does not merely inspire superlatives—it *is* a living superlative."

Whales are amazing for many reasons, not least because of their almost unbelievable hugeness. Blue whales are far larger than any other living creatures—and about three times as big as the biggest dinosaurs ever were. The weight of a single blue whale is equal to that of two thousand human beings, its length equivalent to four city buses end to end.

Such a huge, mysterious creature arouses both terror and fascination in humans. In times past, however, people were often more fearful than they were curious. The ancient stories about a giant seagoing monster called Leviathan, the biblical tale of Jonah and the "giant fish" that swallowed him, the dreaded white whale in the novel *Moby Dick*—all are examples of humankind's awe of the huge creatures.

Changing perceptions about whales

In part out of fear, and in part because they knew so little about whales, few people in times past saw these great creatures as anything other than terrifying beasts that should be killed whenever possible. They were certainly worth killing, too; humans quickly discovered that whales were rich sources of meat, oil, and other valuable products. People in isolated coastal communities had been killing a few whales every year for thousands of years. But from the mid-1700s until earlier in the twentieth century the practice grew into a well-organized industry, which killed so many of the largest and most valuable whales that several species are today nearly extinct.

Times have changed. The killing of whales for sport or commerce is illegal in the United States; commercial whaling, though still carried on in some parts of the world, is greatly restricted; and the public attitude toward the huge mammals has moved from fear and indifference to curiosity and affection. This shift in the way people think about whales has taken place primarily because both advances in whale studies and the impact of the environmental movement have provided new insights into the ways whales live and die.

Whalers sink their lances into a gigantic sperm whale in an 1890 engraving. The mass hunting of whales, which continued into the twentieth century, threatened the survival of several species of these animals.

Researchers know that whales are capable of violent behavior if threatened, and some species are a threat to other sea creatures (particularly the orca, which earned the nickname "killer whale" because it will attack seals, sea lions, and even other whales). But they now know that whales can also be friendly and playful. They know that whales are generally peaceful creatures that take care of their young, do not disturb animals other than the ones they seek for food, and often come to the defense of other whales in danger.

Another aspect of whale research has made them especially appealing to humans: the mounting evidence that whales are intelligent. For instance, whales generally live in highly organized social groups, a behavior that indicates a degree of intelligence. They use a sophisticated radarlike technique to navigate during their long seasonal migrations. And they communicate with each other in a complex sonic language that scientists do not yet understand. The question of whale intelligence is still being studied.

Many conservationists, however, say that whether a creature is or is not intelligent does not matter. People should care about whales, they argue, simply because these wild animals are in danger of disappearing from the planet forever.

Whales and the web of life

Conservationists have been concerned for a long time about the need to protect wild animals and the habitats they live in. For many years, however, the general public did not pay close attention. It is only in the last twenty-five years that the environmental movement has raised public awareness about ecology, emphasizing the fragility of the earth and the need to conserve its remaining resources and species. Endangered whales, through the campaign that became known as Save the Whales, have been the most prominent symbols of this increased public awareness.

Recent efforts to protect whales and help them thrive have had some effect, but in general these populations are still in grave danger. First whaling decreased the numbers of some species to virtually zero, and now another man-made problem—pollution of the oceans—is posing a new and perhaps even more dangerous threat. As Nigel Bonner, a British expert on marine mammals, states, "Although no cetacean species has become extinct in the last thousand years, it cannot be much more than a decade or so before this becomes no longer true."

Despite this dismal prediction, however, there are a few encouraging signs. Pacific gray whales, for instance, have recently made a strong comeback from near-extinction; to a lesser degree, so have right whales. The scientific study of whales has also made great progress in recent years. By learning more about these strange, fascinating creatures—for example, by researching such questions as why gray whales have reappeared since protection began while other species have not—scientists hope to find ways to allow all the whales to survive indefinitely.

1

The Basics About Whales

WHALES ARE OFTEN mistaken for fish. It is easy to make this mistake; after all, both fish and whales have fins and tails, and both live in the water. But there are many differences between the two kinds of marine animals.

The biggest difference is that whales are mammals. This means that they are warm-blooded creatures and that they breathe air. Indeed, whales must regularly come to the surface for air because they do not have gills like those that let a fish breathe underwater. Furthermore, whales do not lay eggs but give birth to live young, called calves, which they nurture with milk.

The birth process

The birth process in whales is relatively long compared with other mammals. Gestation (pregnancy) takes ten to sixteen months, depending on the species. Most female whales give birth only every two or three years, though some, such as grays and humpbacks, can give birth two years in a row. Almost always, just one calf is born at a time. Young whales grow quickly: a newborn blue whale weighs over two tons and will reach twice that weight within the first week.

Most species of whales prefer to travel to coastal waters, shallow lagoons, or warm-water inlets to give birth. This phenomenon has been noted for a very long time. In the first century A.D., the writer Pliny the Elder described

the behavior of northern right whales by saying, "They do not appear in the [warm] Ocean of Cadiz until winter, and for a fixed period of time they hide in an open, peaceful bay and there deliver their young."

No one knows exactly the life expectancy of whales, but scientists have made guesses based on information about other mammals. "In general," Jacques-Yves Cousteau explains, "mammals reach sexual maturity when they have lived out 15 percent of their life expectancy." Assuming that rule holds for whales—something that is yet to be confirmed—the French marine explorer created predictions that include an estimated life span for sei and minke whales of 20 to 25 years; for rights, fins, and bowheads of 40; for grays of 50 to 60; blues, 35 to 40; humpbacks, 45 to 50; and sperm whales, 70.

A killer whale and its mother swim side by side. Mother whales keep their young close by for at least a year after birth.

Types of whales

The scientific naming of animals uses divisions and subdivisions to identify specific creatures. These names are in Latin. The term "cetaceans" refers to the large category (called an order) that includes whales, dolphins, and porpoises. The order Cetacea is further divided into two suborders: Odontoceti and Mysticeti. Each of these suborders is divided still further into genera (the plural of "genus") and species.

"Odontoceti" means "toothed whales." As the name indicates, these whales have teeth, which they use for seizing and chewing food. Among the toothed whale species are sperm whales, bottle-nosed whales, beluga whales, orca whales, and narwhals. Toothed whales usually eat smaller fish and sea creatures, such as squid and octopuses.

Mysticeti, on the other hand, have no teeth. Instead, inside their mouths are huge sheets with rodlike fringes hanging down. To early observers, this bristly material inside a whale's mouth looked like mustaches. In fact, the Latin term means "mustache whales." To a modern observer, Kara Zahn, the effect is "much the same as vertical blinds [that] hang in a window."

The fringe material is called baleen, and whales in this suborder are commonly called baleen whales. Baleen is also sometimes called whalebone, although it resembles flexible cartilage more than real bone.

The Mysticeti, or, in English, mysticetes, use their "mustaches" for eating, filtering enormous quantities of water to strain out food such as fish, shrimp, or the tiny animals and plants called plankton. Depending on the species, a mysticete may have as many as three hundred baleen sheets.

Another identifying factor of some of the larger baleen whales is a series of folds under their throats. These pleats of skin can stretch and expand, allowing the whale to take in more water when feeding. Whales with the pleats are called rorquals, which comes from a Norwegian word meaning "grooved."

Species in the baleen group include blue, fin, humpback, right, pygmy right, and gray whales.

More differences

Besides the difference in mouth structure, baleen and toothed whales can be told apart because baleens have two blowholes for breathing, like the twin nostrils on humans; toothed whales have only a single blowhole.

The differences between whales and their close relatives, porpoises and dolphins, are sometimes very small. Even among cetologists (as scientists who study these creatures are called), there are disagreements over classification.

The primary distinction is size; generally, all cetaceans over twenty feet in length are considered whales. Some dolphins are fairly large, however, and some whales are quite small. Thus there is confusion because, for example, orca whales are considered by many experts to be the largest of the dolphins, not whales at all.

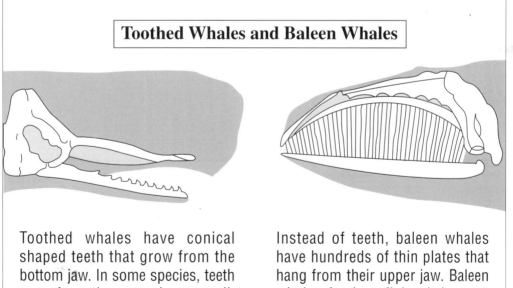

Toothed Whales and Baleen Whales

Toothed whales have conical shaped teeth that grow from the bottom jaw. In some species, teeth grow from the upper jaw as well. Toothed whales feed on fish, squid, and octopus.

Instead of teeth, baleen whales have hundreds of thin plates that hang from their upper jaw. Baleen whales feed on fish, shrimp, or plankton, which is filtered from the water through their baleen plates.

Born to swim

According to current evolutionary thought, whales, dolphins, and porpoises are distantly related to present-day hoofed animals. One theory is that these animals' common ancestor was a wolf-sized creature that lived about 60 million years ago and hunted fish along the shores of oceans. According to this theory, some of these creatures eventually moved into the sea full-time.

Over time, their legs gradually changed into flippers and tails, their nasal openings moved to the tops of their heads for easier breathing at the surface, and their form smoothed out to become as efficient as possible for traveling in the water.

Many other changes came about as well, as whales adapted over centuries to their watery world. "Most of the distinguishing traits we see today," says writer Kara Zahn, "are the result of adaptations to environmental conditions and to exploit [make use of] a given resource."

For instance, because a water creature can support more weight than an animal that depends on its legs, whales can be much larger than creatures that live on land. This is why scientists say that there were no dinosaurs substantially larger than the largest known fossils. As Zahn explains:

> [T]he dinosaur's ability to bulk up was limited by his bone structure. Because of this structural deficiency, a dinosaur's limbs would snap beneath the strain of too much weight. . . . The whale's skeletal system on the other hand developed primarily to insure speed and motion [in] the ocean.

Adaptations

Another example of adaptation is one that helps whales stay warm even in near-freezing temperatures. Virtually all mammals meet this challenge with a layer of hair or fur. Fur would slow down swimmers, however, so whales have instead a layer of fat, called blubber, as thick as twenty inches.

The necessity to breathe air might seem like a drawback for a creature that lives in the sea. After all, having to surface just to breathe affects a whale's ability to swim or

dive for long periods. However, whales have adapted to this situation by evolving a system that lets them breathe more efficiently than land mammals.

A human typically clears only about 15 percent of the air in his or her lungs with a single breath. A whale, however, gets rid of 90 percent of the air in its lungs with each breath. This means that whales can swim for a long time between breaths and can stay underwater for long periods. When whales do surface to breathe, in an action called "breaching," it is a dramatic sight. Whales expel huge plumes of air and water, visible from a far distance, out of blowholes at the top of their heads.

Another adaptation in whales that allows them to remain submerged for many minutes involves myoglobin, a substance in mammalian muscle tissues that makes it possible to store extra oxygen. Very high concentrations of myoglobin in their muscles allow whales to maintain especially high oxygen levels in their systems, even when swimming deeply and for long periods.

The depth to which a whale dives depends on its species, since different species look for different kinds of

Providing a spectacular sight, a humpback whale breaches to fill its lungs with air. When the whale exhales it will produce a huge spout of air and water out of the blowholes at the top of its head.

food. Some whales normally dive to only about 160 feet, while others, such as sperm whales, descend regularly to 1,500 feet and have been found entangled in cables at nearly 4,000 feet below the surface.

Protecting endangered species

The term "endangered" has a specific meaning. It is connected to a U.S. law, the Endangered Species Act (ESA), which was passed by Congress in 1973. The ESA, along with international regulations also passed in the 1970s, expanded and strengthened the poorly enforced policies that the International Whaling Commission had designed in the 1930s to protect right and bowhead whales.

According to the ESA's guidelines, whales as well as other species could be listed as either threatened or endangered if their numbers diminished and extinction was imminent. The terms "endangered" and "threatened" are defined in a special edition of the National Marine Fisheries Service journal *Marine Fisheries Review* devoted to endangered whales:

> Under the Endangered Species Act of 1973, a species is considered "endangered" if it is in danger of extinction throughout all or a significant portion of its range [natural habitat]. A species is considered "threatened" if it is likely to become endangered in the foreseeable future.

Seventy-seven species of cetaceans have been identified so far. New species are still being discovered, and there is no reason to think that scientists have found them all. Five new species of toothed whales alone have been identified in the last forty years.

Today, a few of these species are in danger of disappearing primarily because whale hunting significantly reduced their populations. The species now considered endangered are the right, bowhead, blue, fin, sei, humpback, and sperm whales. The gray whale was once considered endangered, but in 1994 it was removed from the list of endangered species because its population had risen to the point of allowing researchers to declare that the species is stable.

Right whales become endangered

The right whale was the first whale species to be so widely hunted that it came close to extinction. Ever since man began seriously hunting whales, the right whale has been the first choice. The effect was, predictably, a serious decline in numbers; as Cousteau notes, "Populations of right whales have been reduced since the late eighteenth century."

Right whales are so named because whalers in the last century discovered that they were the "right" whales to look for. These slow-moving and unassertive creatures float when killed instead of sinking into the sea, and they swim relatively close to shore. They were therefore the easiest of all the whales to capture. Also, right whales were especially rich sources of oil, meat, and other valuable materials.

No one knows exactly how many right whales once swam in the oceans, but the number is thought to be in the tens or even hundreds of thousands. Whalers sought and

A right whale's seven-yard-wide tail plunges into the water as the whale dives off the coast of Brazil. Because right whales are slow-moving and therefore easy to kill, they became the first species hunted to near extinction.

captured the species so easily that the threat of extinction arose very quickly. In the early 1800s, for instance, 14,000 right whales were taken every year in the region around New Zealand alone; by 1935, the annual catch in that same area was four.

At the turn of the century, there were probably no more than a few dozen right whales worldwide, and today it is estimated that only about a thousand survive, primarily in the North Pacific and the waters off Nova Scotia, Argentina, and South Africa. Right whales have been protected from hunting since the 1930s. For unknown reasons, however, right whales have shown no sign of making a recovery despite their protection.

Although it was the International Whaling Commission that first accorded right whales protection, the ESA and its global kin maintain the right whales' endangered status.

Bowheads and blues become endangered

Unlike other whale species, many of which travel great distances during their annual migrations from spring and summer breeding grounds to winter feeding areas, bowhead whales live in the far northern Arctic all year round.

Because the species was intensely hunted in years past, there are no bowheads at all in the eastern Arctic. The only survivors are in the western Arctic, mostly between Siberia and Alaska. The worldwide bowhead population before hunting was probably about 50,000 animals. Now it is estimated that only 3,000 to 4,000 survive. Like the right whale, the bowhead has been protected since the 1930s but shows no signs of recovering. No one is sure why this is so.

As with other species of whales that were hunted extensively, scientists can only guess how many blue whales existed before commercial whaling began. They estimate, however, that blues once numbered in the hundreds of thousands. By the beginning of the twentieth century, whaling had reduced that figure to only a few hundred.

Today, the number of blue whales has risen, to an estimated 12,000. Despite this comeback, the species is still considered endangered. As Cousteau concludes,

[E]ven cetologists not given to dire [pessimistic] predictions believe that it will take blue whales at least 50 years to recover to only half of the preexploitation population—and that is assuming a total suspension of all whaling. A half-century, and provided there are no hitches!

Humpbacks and sperm whales become endangered

Humpbacks were hunted more extensively than any other baleen whale because they yield so much oil relative to their size. They were not the best catch as far as whalers were concerned. When the choicest whales were gone, however, they became the designated prey. "Humpbacks were far from being the 'right' whales to kill; they were usually skinny, had negligible baleen, and sank when they were killed," according to writer Richard Ellis. "Nevertheless, the whalers picked them off whenever and wherever they found them."

Humpbacks were widely hunted until they gained protected status in 1966. The North Atlantic population, which once was probably about 5,000, was almost completely wiped out by 1915. Other stocks of humpbacks survive in the Pacific and the Antarctic; but in the Antarctic alone, nearly 150,000 were killed between the beginning of the twentieth century and 1966. Estimates for the current worldwide population range widely, from 1,500 to 10,000.

The sperm whale is the only one of the great whales—the hugest of the huge—that has teeth rather than baleen. Hundreds of thousands of sperm whales may still swim in the ocean. Apparently there are roughly as many sperm whales today as there were when these whales were plentiful. No other species of large whale has survived as well.

Current estimates for the worldwide sperm whale population range from 60,000 to over 300,000. This might seem like a lot, but many scientists fear that the figure is misleading. The whales are divided into small, isolated groups that, individually, may be below the sustainable level; in other words, some groups are so small that they cannot reproduce fast enough to maintain adequate numbers. No one knows yet whether the sperm whale population will be

Recent efforts to protect whales have had some effect, though many species remain in danger of extinction.

able to rise to the level it once enjoyed. They were given international protection in 1981.

Endangered smaller whales

The right, bowhead, blue, humpback, and sperm whales were the most valuable and easily caught of all the whale species. These were, therefore, the first to be hunted. Yet, as whalers found it increasingly difficult to locate these species, they began to hunt smaller varieties. As Nigel Bonner writes, "Whale killing is not confined to the great whales, or even to commercial killing."

The first of the smaller species to be regularly sought was the fin whale. Known as "razorbacks" because of the sharp fins on their dorsal, or top, side, these whales once numbered in the hundreds of thousands. Estimates of current fin whale populations vary widely, but there are probably about 120,000 left, mostly in the Southern Hemisphere.

As with the fin whale, the hunting of sei whales began relatively late, in about 1960, after the more desirable species were nearly gone. Very little is known about the size of the preexploitation population of sei whales, or even about their present numbers. Cousteau gives a general estimate for the entire sei population in the North Atlantic of about 3,000, suggesting that the original, or North Pacific, population was between 50,000 and 60,000. Today there may be no more than 18,000 left. Similarly, it is generally acknowledged that there are only 70,000 to 75,000 sei whales south of the equator today, in contrast to a preexploitation population size of 130,000 to 300,000 in the Southern Hemisphere.

Both fin and sei whales have been recognized as endangered by various organizations since the 1970s. Hunting of these two species, however, did not diminish until 1986 when the International Whaling Commission issued a ban on catching endangered whales.

Natural causes and predators

Like all animals, whales are subject to death by natural causes. Fatal sicknesses or injuries due to their own physical makeup, or to attack by other animals, add significantly to the man-made dangers that are threatening them with extinction.

A U.S. Coast Guard officer stands by a beached fin whale as it lifts its tail and flukes in shallow waters off the Oregon coast.

Whale calves, like all young animals, are especially vulnerable to disease. Steve Swartz, a researcher and an expert on gray whales, has estimated that nearly 6 percent of newborn grays born in the coastal lagoons of Baja California die in infancy from various natural causes. Many of the calves that do survive are not strong enough to withstand the long springtime migration in the open sea. About one-third of the calves born in Baja California lagoons die before their groups reach southern California.

Even as adults, whales are susceptible to disease. Cetologists have determined a number of causes of natural deaths among whales, including cancer, pneumonia, jaundice, and arthritis, as well as stomach ulcers and heart disease.

Larger species, such as blues and humpbacks, are so enormous that they are generally safe from natural predators—that is, other animals that hunt. But smaller whales must always be on their guard. For instance, beluga whales swim in river mouths and estuaries in the Northern

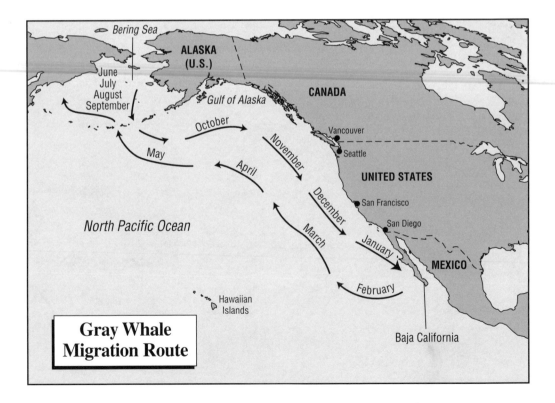

Gray Whale Migration Route

Hemisphere, and they must constantly beware of attack by polar bears, which will paddle out in the water and overcome stray belugas.

Even when smaller whales swim farther from land, they are threatened—in this case by sharks and orca whales, which are often nicknamed killer whales. Orcas are beautiful and fascinating, but they can be dangerous to other sea creatures. Fish and small mammals like seals, dolphins, and porpoises are their main prey, but they will also go after larger prey—including the less massive whales.

All animals, including whales, face disease and predators. These conditions alone cannot explain why whales are endangered. "Great size . . . does not always guarantee longevity for the whales," according to humpback whale researcher Cynthia D'Vincent. "They have few natural enemies, [and] this predation is insignificant when compared to that of man."

Strandings

Another danger for whales is also one of the greatest mysteries in the entire animal kingdom: the phenomenon of stranding. Stranding occurs when whales—either singly or in groups, and for no apparent reason—beach themselves and die. Despite countless studies, no one knows why whales become stranded. As writer Tim Dietz notes, "For years scientists have been struggling with the answers to [this question], but to date all they've been able to come up with is theories."

Certain species of whales seem more likely to strand than others. Barry Lopez, a distinguished natural history writer, notes that "[i]t is almost always toothed whales that [strand], most commonly pilot whales, Atlantic white-sided dolphins, false killer whales, and sperm whales—none of which are ordinarily found close to shore." The sperm whale is the only endangered species that regularly strands itself.

For unknown reasons, gray whales appear to be capable of surviving strandings better than other species. Occasionally, grays run aground if they are caught in shallow

A volunteer throws a bucket of sea water over a pod of pilot whales stranded on Squaw Island in the Atlantic. The reason whales become stranded continues to mystify researchers.

water at low tide, but because of their shape they are usually able to support themselves long enough to float free on the next tide.

Many theories have been put forward to explain stranding. Some experts blame parasitic infestations in the inner ear, which may disorient and confuse whales by impairing their echolocation (the process by which they home in on objects they cannot see). Other theories that have been put forward involve attempts at escape: from storms, loud underwater sounds, attacks from predators, the effects of pollution, or harassment from human observers or hunters.

Still another theory suggests that ill whales, sensing they do not have the strength to swim and surface repeatedly, seek shallow water where they can rest and breathe easily. Some experts propose, meanwhile, that mass strandings result from a form of panic attack, noting that many herd animals are prone to seemingly senseless behavior. According to this theory, if the leader of one of the whale groups that have especially strong social bonds goes off in a strange direction, the other whales will follow blindly, like stampeding cattle.

One part of the mystery concerns whales that sometimes stubbornly return to shore even when returned to open water by humans. An answer to this question may lie in the current theory that whales navigate by sensing variations in the intensity of the earth's magnetic field. If this is true, then regions of unusually high or low magnetic energy would disorient whales from their customary routes, causing them to blunder into shallow water and strand before they are able to achieve reorientation. "The implication," according to British cetologist Anthony R. Martin, "is that the animals were following these lines of [magnetic] force, in the same way that we can follow the height contours of a hill while walking, and simply blundered into the coastline where it intercepted the magnetic contour."

Strandings, predators, and other natural phenomena are not the reasons for whales' endangered status. There are many other causes for the scarcity of whales of so many species. All the major contributors to the modern plight of whales have been human activities. The single worst human factor was a large, complex business—the commercial whaling industry—that until recently thrived on large-scale killing of the giant animals.

2

The Hunt
for Whales

FOR MOST OF the thousands of years that humans have hunted whales, the number captured was so small that no species was in danger of extinction. Primitive villages and small coastal communities were lucky to kill one or two whales a year—just enough to satisfy their needs for food and oil. The whales were therefore able to reproduce fast enough to maintain their large populations and thrive in the open seas.

That stable arrangement changed within a short period, namely, the age of intense commercial whaling that began with the European whalers of the eighteenth century and ended only recently. Each new development—Yankee whaling ships, early mechanized inventions such as the harpoon gun, and the enormous, self-contained "floating cities" used in modern whaling—increased the ability of people in the industry to hunt quickly and efficiently.

To whalers of the early days of the industry, the concept of treating their prey sensitively or conservatively was alien. As writer Tim Dietz notes,

> To the majority of 19th-century whaling captains, the idea of studying their prey would be akin to a grocer studying his grapefruit. Whales were viewed as nothing more than products, something to be harvested as efficiently as possible, with minimal damage to ships and men.

Whaling thrived with this attitude until the 1970s, and then began to die out. Today the industry is more or less

gone, and, although a small amount of whaling is still done by a few countries, including Japan and Norway, huge whaling fleets no longer exist.

Hunted too much

The most desired species of whales were hunted until there were too few left to bother with. Only then, earlier in the twentieth century, was any serious thought given to protection. No one, at least no one in a position to act, considered whales to be anything other than gigantic, waterborne sources of money, ripe for the taking. Those who exploited whales did not think about conserving their resource until it was too late. As Richard Ellis, an artist and writer who specializes in sea creatures, concludes, "We must assume that the [early] whalers believed their prey to represent an inexhaustible [never-ending] natural resource. But we must also realize that the whaling industry learned almost nothing from its own experience."

A large hook on a nineteenth-century whaling ship rips the flesh from a whale. At the time, whales were a profitable source of food and oil, and as more efficient hunting methods were developed, the whaling industry flourished.

Nor was much consideration given to sparing female whales and calves, a form of conservation that would have guaranteed continued whaling in the future. The whalers routinely killed females and young whales, with no thought to the need to replenish the populations. Because of this shortsighted practice, some species remain in grave danger and may not survive. As Ellis notes:

> The story of commercial whaling has been a story of unrelieved greed and insensitivity. In no other activity has our species practiced such a relentless pursuit of wild animals, and if no whale species has become extinct at the hands of the whalers, it has not been for want of trying.

Early whaling

Shore-dwelling people in ancient times must have watched in wonder as whales spouted and swam in the sea. When dead whales washed up, or live ones were beached, these communities must have quickly realized that they had received gifts of valuable meat and oil. It probably did not take long for them to begin actively hunting whales.

Native Americans on both coasts, Eskimos, Basques in Spain and France, and the Japanese and Norwegians were among the earliest whalers. Each of these peoples had legends and customs associated with whales. The Basques were probably responsible for the legend of Leviathan, a monster that was part whale and part serpent, four acres wide and covered with treelike growths and barnacles. Indians in the Pacific Northwest, meanwhile, performed elaborate rituals before and after each hunt, asking forgiveness from the whale and welcoming its spirit into the community.

All these communities, in the early days, practiced subsistence whaling; that is, the meat and oil were consumed locally. Methods differed from place to place, but typically early whalers used small, open boats to chase the whales and harpoons or lances to kill them.

By the sixteenth century, the Basques had perfected their techniques, killing all the right whales close to their homes. They then ventured across the Atlantic to find new prey. Remains of a Basque whaling station from this period have been found in Canada, on the coast of Labrador. By this time, the Basque operation was no longer strictly subsistence whaling. The products they collected on their far-flung expeditions were sold all over Europe. By the next century, other countries also had extensive whaling fleets.

The great explorations in the eighteenth century opened up huge new territories for European whalers. When Captain James Cook explored the Antarctic in 1774, for instance, he found enormous numbers of right, blue, sei, and fin whales. During this period, the American whaling fleet—the famous Yankee whaling ships—also came into being.

Early whalers cut up a whale pulled from monster-infested waters in this sixteenth-century woodcut.

The golden age of whaling

Shortly after America became a nation, the new country dominated the whaling industry. The ports of New England, such as Nantucket, New Bedford, and Mystic, became the world's biggest whaling centers, and for most of the 1800s the majority of the world's whaling ships flew the American flag. In 1842 there were 652 American whaling ships; the rest of the world could muster a total of only 230 vessels.

Yankee whaling reached its peak around 1876, when 735 American vessels plied the oceans. One of the most important novels in American literature, *Moby Dick*, is set aboard a fictional Yankee whaler during this era; its author, Herman Melville, was a former whaling man.

Yankee whaling was so extensive and well organized that it soon killed off most of the whales along the American coast. Indeed, by the mid–eighteenth century, there were so few right whales in New England's waters that the Yankees had to look to the Pacific and the South Atlantic. The New Englanders also began looking for species that so far had been ignored. Sperm whales were considered by many to be the next best thing to the right whale because their enormous heads contain a huge amount of spermaceti oil, the purest of all whale oils. By the 1850s, however, these creatures had become nearly as scarce as right whales, and hunters began chasing less desirable species, such as gray whales.

Crews in small boats would kill a whale with handheld harpoons and haul the carcass, sometimes for miles, back to the main ship. The prey was then "dressed out" (cut up for its contents). Workers flensed (cut away) the animal's blubber, which was thrown into kettles on deck and boiled down into oil.

If the animal was a sperm whale, its intestines would be searched for valuable ambergris. If the quarry was a mysticete, its baleen would be salvaged. Everything else—including the meat—was left in the sea for sharks to eat. The Japanese have long considered whale meat a delicacy, but few other cultures troubled themselves to save it.

What the whalers took

Oil was the primary objective of the whale hunters. Although spermaceti oil from sperm whales was especially prized for its purity, other species were also rich in oil. Whale oil was used for lamp fuel and for many other purposes, including the manufacture of dynamite and the lubrication of machinery.

Whalebone, the baleen plates of mysticetes, was used much as plastic is used today, in products requiring strength and flexibility. Whalebone served in an amazing variety of items, including buggy whips, umbrella ribs, chairs, mattresses, store shutters, brushes, wigs, plumes on soldiers' helmets, and the corset stays and skirt hoops

Nineteenth-century whalers approach their prey from the side as less-fortunate crew members are tossed into the sea after their boat is snapped in half by the whale's forceful tail.

Early whalers off the coast of Long Island "dress out," or cut up, their catch for its contents—oil, whalebone, meat, and ambergris.

popular in women's fashions of the day. It also made short whips that teachers applied to uncooperative schoolchildren; it is still common to say that a person who has taken a beating has gotten "a whaling."

As time went on, uses were found for other parts of the animal as well. Once European and Yankee whalers discovered the Japanese market for whale meat, following the opening of Japan to the West in the 1860s, meat became one of the most profitable parts of the catch. A whale's liver is a rich source of vitamin A, and other organs were used for medicines, soaps, and cosmetics. The teeth of odontocetes were made into piano keys or scrimshaw, the decorative items carved by sailors to pass the time on long voyages.

The bones were ground into meal and sold as animal food or fertilizer. The skin was made into leather and the muscle tendons were used for tennis racquet strings and for sewing up surgical incisions. In Scandinavian fishing villages, the translucent intestines sometimes even substituted for glass in windows.

Such products from whales were vital to industry in the last century—as important then as petroleum products are now. Many of the plastic or oil-based materials common today replace substances once obtained from whales.

The rarest but most valuable item of all was ambergris, which is still used as an ingredient in perfumes. No one knows exactly what creates this waxy substance, which is found in the intestines of sperm whales. One theory is that it forms around the undigested beaks of squids, in the same way that a pearl forms around a speck of sand inside an oyster. As writer Tim Dietz notes in his book *Whales and Man,*

> There were even stories of entire whaling voyages being abandoned after the crew discovered a large chunk of the valuable concretion [substance]. In 1912, a near-bankrupt whaling company found the largest chunk ever—weighing 1,003 pounds—which sold for more than $60,000, saving the company.

Whaling moves into the modern age

Before the end of the nineteenth century, vast deposits of crude oil had been discovered in the earth. By the early part of this century, the petroleum industry was beginning to replace whaling as the source of oil and other products. Also, whalers had killed off so many whales that expeditions were becoming increasingly expensive and decreasingly profitable.

It seemed as though the whaling industry might die off. But then whaling was saved by a series of technological innovations.

Early in the nineteenth century, James Watt's perfection of the steam engine allowed shipbuilders to switch from sailing ships to powered steamships. These new vessels almost completely replaced the huge commercial sailing ships because enormous engines allowed the steamers to travel greater distances faster, and with greater safety and reliability.

Before the arrival of the steamship, whalers had been limited in the scope of their hunts. The availability of machine-powered vessels, however, gave rise to a new type of whaling: pelagic, or deep-sea, whaling. Whalers could now hunt deep-sea species like blue whales, which had been largely ignored because they lived too far from shore factories to be hunted effectively.

The harpoon gun and the slipway

The most destructive period in the history of the industry began in 1868, when a Norwegian whaler, Svend Foyn, perfected a design for an explosive harpoon that could be fired from a cannon. The harpoon penetrated deep into the vital organs of the whale and exploded, bringing death far more quickly and efficiently than the old method of using handheld spears and harpoons. As Richard Ellis observes, "The whale had as much of a fighting chance as a tree had against a chain saw."

But most dead whales still had to be artificially filled with air to keep them from sinking. Then the whale carcasses had to be processed while floating beside the ship (a wasteful and inefficient chore) or slowly and tediously hauled to a factory onshore. The innovation that made both these unsatisfactory processes obsolete was the stern slipway, a massive chute, designed into the rear, or stern, of a large ship. This invention, the brainchild of another Norwegian whaler, Peter Sørlle, enabled workers to pull huge whale carcasses onto the decks of ships, for complete and relatively convenient processing at sea. Enormous new ships, called factory ships, were built to accommodate the new technique, which Sørlle introduced in 1925, only a few years before some whale species became the subjects of international regulations aimed at protecting them.

The move to the deep sea

As whalers began hunting deep-sea whales that had once been unobtainable, they also hunted some species simply because there were no others to be had.

Massive pieces of whale meat on the slipway of a whaling ship. The slipway was an innovation that allowed whalers to pull the carcasses onto the ships for convenient and efficient processing at sea.

Humpbacks were not very valuable to the early whalers: they were not overly blubbery, and they had poor baleen. Gray whales had also been largely ignored: their baleen plates were small and their meat and oil were inferior. Still, as better-quality whales became scarcer, whalers were reduced to hunting them more frequently. Smaller whales, such as fin and minke whales, were also killed in increasing numbers.

The Antarctic Ocean, the home territory of many of the deep-sea species, became the world's premier whaling ground. Many nations, including Argentina, Denmark,

A worker cuts blubber from the tremendous body of a whale. In the 1930s, as whalers began to realize their supply of whales was dwindling, formal talks about regulating the industry began.

Germany, and Peru, joined the established whaling countries, including Japan, the United States, Norway, Russia, and England, in the search for pelagic whales. Whaling once again was a thriving industry, primarily for meat and, to a lesser extent, for oils and raw materials for cosmetics and manufacturing. In particular, sperm oil was preferred over petroleum products for mechanical lubrication.

The statistics tell the story: in 1910 the annual catch worldwide exceeded 10,000 for the first time; by 1911 that figure had more than doubled. After World War I, the figures continued to increase: 27,000 in 1926, 44,000 in 1931. The industry peaked in 1938, when nearly 55,000 whales were killed worldwide.

Regulating whaling

By the 1930s, it was clear that whalers had a problem. They had become so efficient that they were risking their own jobs by killing off large numbers of whales.

Even before the turn of the century, some experts had warned that the hunting could not continue unrestricted for very long. If the practice continued, the supply of whales surely would shrink to the point of commercial extinction—that is, such a small number of whales would exist that the species would no longer be worth hunting. The whaling companies would then be out of business.

The industry ignored the critical situation, preferring to continue hunting the remaining stocks. In the 1930s, however, formal talks about limiting whaling began. Representatives from most of the whaling countries agreed to protect right and bowhead whales—species that were nearly extinct anyway. They did this by imposing a ban, called a moratorium, on the hunting of these species.

With the idea of allowing whales to reproduce in greater numbers, the whalers also agreed to impose quotas on other species, and to end the common practice of killing female whales accompanied by their young. The number of whales killed would, in theory, be no greater than the number replaced through normal reproduction. If the ideal result, called a "sustained yield," had been achieved, whales would have become a self-renewing resource.

However, this grand plan did not work as hoped. First, several leading whaling nations, including Japan, refused to sign the agreement. The Second World War further delayed legislation to protect whales (although there was almost no whaling during the war, since all available ships were pressed into battle service).

It was not until 1946 that an official regulatory organization was formed: the International Whaling Commission (IWC). That year, the commission added gray whales to the list of whales that were protected from hunting.

The BWU and the IWC

The IWC was designed to implement catch quotas that the whaling industry set for itself. Among the measures whalers put forward was a concept called the blue whale unit (BWU), which was accepted by the industry in the early 1930s and lasted until it was officially dropped in the 1970s.

Originally established by Norwegian whalers and then adopted by the IWC, the BWU was an all-purpose measure meant to be used in judging overall quotas for all species of whales. A blue whale unit (1 BWU) was equivalent to one blue whale, two fin whales, two and a half humpbacks, or six sei whales. That is, each unit consisting of two or more fin, humpback, or sei whales was considered equivalent in oil production to one blue whale. The BWU system was adopted worldwide by the IWC just after World War II. Whalers were allotted a certain number of BWUs per year, but the number varied widely from country to country, depending on the size of a nation's whaling fleet. Between 1945 and 1952 the quota imposed on the world's fleets operating in the Antarctic region was 16,000 BWU.

Little protection for blue whales

Unfortunately, the BWU system took no account of the different degrees to which different stocks of whales were threatened with extinction. It offered no real protection for the species that needed it most, since catching a blue whale took much less effort than was needed to catch six sei whales. But any species of whale is difficult to catch, and whalers logically chose to avoid the extra time, energy, and expense of catching large numbers of smaller whales and instead concentrated on blue whales, filling their quotas and returning to port. Because of the rapid depletion of whale stocks, the BWU quotas were steadily decreased. By 1970, the Antarctic limit of 2,700 BWU was not even achieved by the combined fleets of the whaling nations. Within two years, the BWU system was dropped.

The BWU was an odd concept to put forward for the supposed protection of whales. J. L. McHugh, a former U.S. representative to (and chairman of) the IWC, wrote in his history of the commission, "It should not be necessary to explain why the BWU is illogical as a management unit." Even so, in his book *Men and Whales*, Richard Ellis spells it out, commenting that the BWU "placed a totally unbalanced emphasis on a single species . . . so in the pure name of greed, the early whalers, and later the IWC, by their quotas effectively sentenced the blue whale to extinction."

Little progress

Overall, the IWC was not an effective organization. Not all the whaling nations joined, and member nations did not necessarily follow its rulings. The commission also was geared to protect the interests of the industry; national representatives were generally sympathetic to the whalers, not the whales. Furthermore, each country fiercely protected its own interests, rather than trying to see the situation from a global perspective. And the commission was secretive about its actions, effectively barring independent parties from participating in or even observing its meetings.

Furthermore, enforcing the BWU quotas was virtually impossible. Often, various national governments turned a blind eye to illegal whaling practices. It has been estimated, for instance, that between 1948 and 1987 Soviet whalers killed at least a hundred thousand whales over and above national quotas, while the government of the USSR did nothing to stop them. "No one wanted to restrict [the whaling activity]," according to Ernst Cherny, a former Soviet whaler. "They killed females, calves, illegal species, at illegal times, in illegal whaling zones, and all of it was done because the government sanctioned [approved] . . . these global violations."

The Soviet Union was not the only country to exceed its quotas. Many illegal catches by Japan, Korea, Norway, Iceland, and other countries were documented, as well.

The international movement to save the whales began in earnest in the early 1970s, but many years passed before the IWC began to respond. Sperm whales were added to the commission's protected list in 1981, joining right and bowhead whales. Then, in 1986, the IWC declared a worldwide moratorium on commercial hunting of blue, fin, gray, sei, and humpback whales. However, IWC rulings did not affect several nonmember countries with whaling industries. Thus Portugal, Somalia, Chile, South

WHALE, n
large body,
long spine,
big brain.

INTERNATIONAL WHALING COMMISION, n
small body,
no spine,
no brains.

ROTHCO

© Raeside/Rothco. Reprinted with permission.

Korea, and China continued to catch protected species, and even member nations occasionally violated the ban.

Since its establishment some sixty years ago, the IWC has proved to be slow, shortsighted, cumbersome, and ineffective. The commission still meets today, though its actions are even less helpful to whale survival than before. Its main focus is the protection of the interests of the remnants of the whaling industry, although some emphasis on environmental concerns has appeared.

Today a combination of factors has virtually abolished the whaling industry. One reason is simple economics: whales are scarce, and whaling is no longer very profitable. Another reason is that almost all the products that once came from whales can now be obtained elsewhere—cultivated in plants or manufactured synthetically. Still another is the intense international movement to save the whales that began in the 1970s and brought tremendous pressure to bear on politicians and diplomats.

The number of nations that gave up whaling slowly grew. American whaling stopped with the passage of the Marine Mammal Protection Act in 1972. Many other nations with smaller whaling fleets also abandoned the industry. The biggest commercial fleets that continued into the 1970s, those of the Soviet Union and Japan, ceased openly commercial operations in 1987 and 1988, respectively.

It is now illegal to import whale products into America and much of Europe. However, Japan still consumes whale meat, supplied by whalers in several countries, including Chile, Peru, the Philippines, and South Korea, that are not members of the IWC. Environmentalists sometimes term this practice pirate whaling, since it operates outside the bounds of international law.

Pirate whaling

Conservationists protest that besides hunting in ways that are contrary to the regulations of the IWC, the so-called pirate whaling operations are especially cruel and wasteful. The use of nonexplosive harpoons, a new version of an ancient hunting weapon, protects the meat but means a slow, painful death for the animal. Moreover, it is not uncommon to find that a fifty-ton whale has been killed for only two tons of prime cuts of meat.

Governments of nations not belonging to the IWC continue to turn a blind eye toward violations of the commission's regulations, and in any event, it is impossible to enforce such limits effectively in the vast reaches of the ocean. As Cousteau wryly remarks, "Harpooning a protected whale is less risky than shoplifting cosmetics made of whale oil."

Complicating matters further, parties who object to pirate whaling generally lack the standing to bring suit in international courts. Thus few organizations that can afford to do so are willing to commit the funds necessary to send ships to monitor suspected violators of IWC bans. Also daunting is the prospect of asking unarmed crews to get close enough to a hostile vessel to videotape the killing of whales. For the people doing the killing strongly feel that they have every right to make a living in this way.

Aboriginal whaling

A special case has been made by the IWC concerning whaling by certain aboriginal peoples—descendants of the first known inhabitants of a given region. The aboriginal tribes no longer really need to hunt whales for food. However, they maintain that the act of whaling is an important part of their cultural heritage. Whaling has been a significant factor in aboriginal life for thousands of years, and the people protest that to give it up would mean losing a crucial piece of their ethnic identity.

The Eskimos of Greenland, as a result of this argument, are allowed to hunt limited amounts of minke whales, belugas, narwhals, and humpbacks, using traditional tools and methods such as sealskin canoes and handheld harpoons. Eskimos in Alaska can also catch a limited number of bowheads, though they use more modern technology. The Alaskan hunt has been sharply criticized, since bowheads are perhaps the most endangered of all the large whales. The Alaskan natives, however, say that they want to be able to take only a few every year, and they emphasize that responsibility for the near-extinction of the bowheads lies with Yankee whalers.

Recently, the Makah tribe of Washington State requested permission to resume hunting gray whales, a practice they had maintained for hundreds of years before abandoning it in 1926 as the species became endangered. But the new request, for five gray whales annually, has generated an international controversy and the outcome is uncertain.

Some Makah leaders rely on the argument that whaling was an important part of the tribe's identity. According to Lawrence Watters, who teaches coastal resources law at Lewis and Clark College in Portland, Oregon, "You shouldn't underestimate the spiritual and cultural significance of whaling to this tribe. It's a basic identity, like

Because whaling is an important part of their cultural heritage, certain aboriginal groups, such as these Greenland Eskimos, are allowed to hunt a limited amount of whales.

baseball or the right to drive cars in [modern] America." On the other hand, several elderly Makah members have objected to the hunt, saying that it is simply commercial. "There is no spiritual training going on," they state in ads placed in local newspapers. "Our people haven't used or had whale meat/blubber since the early 1900s." In mid-1996, amid a storm of local and international protest, the Makah tribe temporarily withdrew its request.

Other dangers from fishermen

Fishermen who are not whalers sometimes pose another threat to whales. Some species of whales, especially the smaller ones, eat the same fish harvested by commercial fishermen as food for humans. Since whales often are more efficient in this competition for the same food source, a healthy whale population may diminish the supply of species eaten by people.

During the 1930s, for instance, Canadian fishermen blamed their poor salmon and cod catches on the St. Lawrence beluga whales. The Quebec government authorized aerial bombing of the whales, and a bounty was paid for each dead whale. Thousands of belugas were killed before environmentalists succeeded in passing a law outlawing the hunt.

Sometimes, fishermen affect whales in other ways. Overfishing, for example, occurs when a particular type of fish has been caught by commercial fishermen until that species is almost gone. If a species that whales rely on is overfished, the whales are forced to search elsewhere.

British research scientist Peter G. H. Evans notes two typical instances of dwindling whale populations due to overfishing of other species:

> The collapse of energy-rich herring stocks may have played some part in the virtual absence of cetaceans in the southern part of the North Sea (even though other factors such as pollution may be more important). The . . . collapse of capelin [small smeltlike fish] stocks in the late 1970s [in Canada] is considered [to have had] a negative effect on fin whales.

In such cases, the whales probably do not die—they simply migrate elsewhere to find other food sources—but they have disappeared from their home region, probably for good.

Accidental entrapment

Another danger is posed by nets laid out for noncetaceous sea animals. Off such heavily fished areas as New England and eastern Newfoundland, many humpbacks, minke whales, and occasionally right and fin whales have been accidentally entrapped by nets. This problem arose primarily in the 1970s, when several species of offshore whales began feeding closer to land. The reasons are unclear, but it may be that overfishing in deep waters forced the whales uncustomarily close to shore.

A solution to the problem has been elusive. Modifications in fishing gear, such as acoustic alarms that alert fishermen to the presence of larger creatures, have been only partially successful.

Scientists have also experimented with underwater broadcasting, sending out the sounds made by predatory killer whales in an attempt to scare the unwanted whales away. This technique is expensive and not always successful, however. Even today, as many as 150 whales are trapped each year in the New England–Newfoundland fishing grounds alone, and many die before they can be rescued.

A related problem is created when fishermen lose nets in a storm or throw damaged nets away at sea. Many of the nets are miles long and dozens of yards wide and, since they are made of plastic, they do not degrade. They do not even sink to the bottom; instead, they drift in the

"IF YOU WEREN'T ALWAYS SPOUTING, WE WOULDN'T BE AN ENDANGERED SPECIES!"

© Hoppes/Rothco. Reprinted with permission.

water and become "ghost nets," trapping sea animals of many kinds.

The heads or tails of whales often become so tightly wrapped in lost or discarded commercial fishing nets that the creatures cannot move properly, and they starve, drown, or die of exhaustion. No one knows how many whales die from encounters with ghost nets, but the number may be large despite a moratorium on driftnets declared by the United Nations in 1992.

The aftermath of whaling

To many observers today, the old methods of whaling were cruel, greedy, and insensitive to nature. But the Yankee whalers and other whalers saw whaling simply as taking advantage of a readily available and seemingly endless resource. Only in recent years have some people come to regard whales as animals worth preserving, not just as fuel for industry.

It cannot be denied, however, that the greed and short-sightedness of the whalers seriously threatened the survival of some of the most magnificent animals on earth. The industry's recklessness was self-destructive, since commercial whaling has all but disappeared.

The damage was severe and perhaps permanent. Because of whaling, the survival of many species will be questionable for hundreds of years. They may never recover their former numbers. Industrial whaling is a thing of the past, and it is unlikely to be resumed to any significant degree. But whales face another danger now, one that is also caused by humans: the havoc caused by pollution and habitat destruction.

3

Pollution and Habitat Destruction

AFTER MILLIONS OF years of relatively unthreatened existence, several species of whales were nearly wiped out in just two centuries of whaling. That particular threat is now over, probably for good, but whales still face many other dangers. Chief among these are the man-made forces of pollution and habitat destruction.

Trash in the waters

The earth's oceans are often the final dumping ground for the trash and waste produced by human civilization. The pollution that results from this dumping is the biggest single threat facing whales today.

Direct pollution, which occurs when garbage is tossed overboard from ships, is one form of pollution. According to a 1985 report quoted by writer Kara Zahn, merchant ships alone dump nearly half a million plastic containers into the open sea every day. Unlike toxic chemicals, which tend to remain in one concentrated area, plastic trash will float and spread out over thousands of square miles of open sea. Such trash is regularly found even in such remote waters as the Antarctic, and so it poses a constant threat.

Whales often swallow plastic trash items as they feed. Since this man-made material cannot be digested, it may remain in their bodies, where it is likely to puncture a stomach lining or intestine, or block an animal's eating or breathing apparatus. David List, a spokesman for the U.S.

Marine Commission, remarks that plastic containers are "like individual mines floating around the ocean just waiting for victims."

No one knows exactly how many whale deaths are caused by plastic trash, but some researchers estimate that several hundred animals die each year. As Kara Zahn notes, whales are not the only victims; plastic remnants annually account for "the maiming or deaths of tens of thousands of seabirds, seals, sea lions, and sea otters as well as hundreds of whales, dolphins, porpoises, and sea turtles."

Indirect pollution

A much bigger part of the pollution problem comes from the indirect pollution that results when factories and farms release chemicals into rivers that empty into an ocean. The pollutants in the water contaminate algae and other simple organisms near the bottom of the food chain.

Biologists tow a dead 33-foot whale out from underneath a dock. Although the cause of the whale's death is uncertain, polluted waters may have been a factor.

As these organisms are eaten by animals higher in the chain, the chemicals become increasingly concentrated. Since whales are at the top of the marine food chain, the tissues and organs of whales have the highest concentrations of these toxins.

The size of a particular body of water and its distance from human settlements affect the amount of pollution it experiences. The St. Lawrence estuary and the Mediterranean and the Baltic Seas, because they are small, almost landlocked bodies of water surrounded by areas of industry and highly fertilized agriculture, are among the most polluted. Other areas of heavy pollution include the North Sea, the coast of California, the Gulf of Mexico, and the inland sea of Japan. All these areas are breeding or feeding grounds for many species of whales.

Whales that live and feed on fish and squid in these regions have higher levels of toxins in their bodies than species inhabiting the open seas, such as the Arctic and Pacific Oceans and Antarctic waters. But no waters, even the most remote, are free of traces of pollution. In fact, the highest recorded levels of mercury ever found in cetaceans came from animals in relatively clean waters. These were two killer whales and two false killer whales that became stranded on a remote island off the west coast of Canada in 1993. It is not known, however, how they ingested such large amounts of the deadly heavy metal.

Toxic chemicals

The chemicals that affect whales the most fall into two categories. The first, a group called organochlorines, includes polychlorinated biphenyl (PCBs), which are used in the plastics industry, as well as DDT and other pesticides. (DDT has been banned in the United States but is still used elsewhere.) The second group is made up of heavy metals, such as mercury, lead, zinc, copper, and cadmium, that are used in various industrial processes.

Conclusive proof that these chemicals directly cause cancer, birth defects, or other life-threatening conditions in whales is lacking. The evidence, however, points strongly in that direction, and scientists are worried. As researcher Nigel Bonner notes,

> The discovery of 0.1 part per million of DDT in a whale indicates that it has been exposed to pollution, but it is unlikely that it will be adversely affected by it. On the other hand, much higher levels [have been reported recently] and we can be less sure of the innocuousness [harmlessness] of such levels.

Scientists suspect that high levels of toxins absorbed in the blubber and other parts of whales have sublethal effects; that is, pollutants do not kill the whales outright but affect, among other things, vital aspects of the animals' health, such as their immune systems.

A variety of diseases

Weakened immune systems make whales vulnerable to a variety of diseases ranging from bladder cancer to pneumonia and heart problems. Toxic poisoning may also affect the proper functioning of nervous systems, livers, brains, and other organs. And there is strong evidence that even small amounts of certain chemicals can affect a cetacean's reproductive abilities. If a species of whale cannot breed properly, it will die out.

Oil that leaks from tankers is a serious hazard for seals and other small sea animals, but the effect on whales of this type of pollution is not yet well understood. Some experts feel that whales are not seriously affected by oil slicks on beaches or in the sea. They point out that gray whales sometimes swim directly through oil slicks, apparently without noticing the pollution or trying to avoid it. However, evidence suggests that whales absorb the residue of oil into their respiratory and digestive tracts, where it may affect them later. Oil may clog the baleen bristles of mysticete whales, for instance, and decrease their ability to feed. Also, crude oil ingested by small animals, low on the food chain, may affect whales later, when they feed on the contaminated species.

One intriguing theory links stranding with the effects of pollution. Scientists have yet to amass enough data to prove or disprove this link, but, as Jacques-Yves Cousteau notes, the evidence is strong and "any such abnormality merits investigation."

The study quoted by Cousteau presented evidence of a direct link between contaminants in the western Mediterranean Sea and the death of whales in the region. Lead researcher Diane Viale reported that in addition to the many other kinds of pollution in the region, thousands of tons of toxic chemicals were being dumped every day by a Corsican factory that produced titanium dioxide.

In the two-year period of Viale's research, twenty-four dead or injured whales were reported in the area, compared with a preindustrial average for the same area of two deaths every three years. Viale noted the presence of extremely high levels of pollutants in all the beached whales and concluded, "This increase cannot be ascribed to chance. . . . There could be no escaping the link between

A cleanup worker spreads sheets of paper towels along a Rhode Island harbor in an effort to soak up oil that spilled from a tanker. While the effects of oil absorbed by whales is unknown, some researchers believe that oil may damage the animals' respiratory and digestive tracts.

the increase in the number of whale strandings and the increase in pollution."

Belugas in danger

The most dramatic example of whales endangered by pollution is found on Canada's eastern seaboard, where the St. Lawrence River empties into the Atlantic Ocean. The St. Lawrence estuary, as this region is called, is heavily polluted from power stations, oil rigs, aluminum plants, and other forms of industry upriver.

The region is also the only habitat of beluga whales outside the Arctic. Fossils indicate that the species has been in the area for more than 10,000 years. However, the number of belugas there, which was about 5,000 only a century ago, is now down to about 500. Commercial hunting in the St. Lawrence estuary ended in the 1950s, but the whales have failed to recover.

Although the beluga is not officially listed as endangered, many cetologists are concerned that the St. Lawrence group may soon die out. As writer Tim Dietz notes:

> Recent studies of stranded beluga carcasses show incredible levels of toxins, such as PCBs, DDT, and the insecticide Mirex, in the blubber. These toxins are so deadly that the Canadian Department of Fisheries and Oceans forbids the export of commercial fish with [contamination levels of] 2 parts per million (ppm). Yet the breast milk of one beluga contained an unbelievable 1,725 ppm.

Current knowledge about exactly how pollutants affect whales, and sea creatures in general, has many gaps. Cetologists who are studying the effects of pollution on whales hope the future will bring more attention to the issue. As the World Wildlife Federation states the case in a recent report, *Toxics in Canada's Marine Mammals*: "Toxic contamination of marine mammals' habitat and food supply constitutes a current, ongoing and insidious threat which has not been adequately addressed."

Noise pollution

The increasing amount of noise in the oceans may also be a factor in the reduced well-being of whales. Among the causes of marine noise pollution are large ships' engines, the development of industrial sites on the shoreline, oil exploration, and earthquake research. The noise made by such equipment and activities can travel as far as fifty miles underwater and can reach levels as high as 150 decibels. By comparison, a rock concert rarely gets louder than 100 decibels.

Evidence suggests that noise pollution upsets the delicate sonar, or echolocation, systems that guide some species of whales on their migrations. It may also hamper whales' ability to communicate with one another. Whales are very social animals, and they usually live together in distinct groups called pods. These pods are aided by sophisticated natural sonic communication equipment. Individuals in a group apparently use sound to keep track of each other by making sounds and listening to the sounds produced by others.

However, man-made noise pollution may be affecting the whales' ability to use their bodies' sonar apparatus. Sound travels well underwater, but if the whales' signals are disrupted, it may be difficult or impossible for the animals to find each other. If communication fails and whales are unable to meet during the mating season, they will not reproduce in sufficient numbers to sustain a population.

Studies of how whales react to sound have so far proved inconclusive. In one investigation, a group of bowheads went out of their way to avoid four vessels that were giving off loud signals underwater. In other studies, however, bowheads have shown only mild reactions to similar sounds, indicating merely an increase in breathing rate when the noise level increased. Yet migrating gray whales observed off California in a separate experiment moved close to shore and used the "sound shadow" of rocks to avoid 160-decibel sounds emitted by the research vessels.

Boat traffic

A problem related to noise pollution stems from the increase in recent years in boat traffic, both in the open sea and near shore.

Workers examine the remains of a fin whale that was probably decapitated by a passing ship. With the increase in boat traffic in recent years, reports of ships colliding with whales are not uncommon.

Reports of whales colliding with ships or being injured by propellers are increasingly frequent. These encounters usually do not harm the ships, which may be 250,000-ton supertankers capable of traveling at high speeds. The whales do not fare as well, however; they may receive deep gashes in the back or sides, and occasionally a tail is severed.

The loss of even an entire tail section is not necessarily fatal for a whale, since whales swim by moving their entire bodies. In one study, a gray whale that was completely missing its tail was tracked for nearly 3,500 miles, averaging 40 to 50 miles a day—about half the normal speed.

Some whales, however, suffer life-threatening injuries as a result of collisions with ships. And even if an injury due to a collision is not fatal in itself, it can indirectly result in death. In a number of reported instances, whales were so severely injured that they beached themselves—perhaps to rest and recover—but instead became stranded onshore by a low tide and died.

Habitat destruction

Perhaps the worst aspect of pollution, as far as sea creatures are concerned, is habitat destruction. Habitat destruction is any activity that ruins areas in which animals live, mate, give birth, and feed. Probably the single greatest threat to wildlife throughout the world is the destruction and disturbance of natural habitats by humans.

For sea creatures, these disturbances generally mean changes along the coastline, such as hydroelectric projects and harbor development. Whales are not immune to the dangers posed by habitat destruction. As Peter G. H. Evans writes, "If any cetacean species goes extinct in the next decade or two, it is more likely to be through changes to its habitat than to anything else."

Especially critical for whales are the areas near shore that are used for mating grounds or as rich sources of food. Coastal areas—or wetlands—nurture the growth of algae and flowering plants such as eelgrass. These plants, in turn, provide oxygen in the water, food, and even homes for a wide variety of small marine animals. These smaller animals, which are lower on the food chain, are a major component of the diet of whales.

Any disturbance of a wetlands area, therefore, could have a serious impact on whales later. For instance, small fragments from certain plants that grow in wetlands are swept by currents down to the ocean floor. These fragments are the main source of food for giant squid. Without this nourishment, the giant squid would have died out long ago. Sperm whales, in turn, feed primarily on giant squid, and it is unlikely that if the squid vanished, they could find enough other sources of food for survival.

Many conservationists argue that it is not enough simply to save the whales; it is equally important to preserve the habitats in which they live. A prominent research scientist, Dr. Jim Darling, makes the following statement:

> I think we've convinced most of the world, certainly the western world, that whales should be saved. . . . But probably five percent of the people realize that means you have to save their food supply too. Probably only one percent understand

that saving the food supply means maintaining the integrity of the system which supports the food. Very few people realize that this is all tied together with development. I don't think it's very deep, the understanding, yet the public certainly decides the fate of the animals: there's no question about that.

Disrupting the ecosystem

The species of whales that are most affected by shore development, naturally enough, are those that live close to shore for at least part of the year. Humpback whales, right whales, and gray whales, for instance, use shallow coastal lagoons and bays for breeding. Disturbances of the delicate ecology of these grounds, such as the lagoons of Baja California where gray whales congregate, may have serious effects on the species' capabilities for reproducing.

While offshore oil rigs have destroyed portions of the habitat of some species of whales, there is evidence that the hot water that surrounds the rigs is beneficial to whales because it attracts more fish to the whales' feeding areas.

Offshore oil developments in the Arctic and North Seas have likewise threatened beluga, narwhal, and bowhead populations by destroying certain portions of their territory. On the other hand, there is some evidence that the massive amounts of hot water ejected by offshore oil rigs may actually be beneficial for some whale species, by drawing larger numbers of fish to their feeding areas.

Cousteau is one of many experts who feel that the disruption of ecosystems by development is an even greater threat to whales than pollution. As he and coauthor Yves Paccalet write in their book *Whales:*

> We are dredging new marinas and commercial ports in places where whales have always come to feed, frolic, or breed. . . . New steamship lines, stepped-up urbanization of the coastline, breakneck industrial, residential, and recreational development, airports built out over the water, marinas, offshore drilling rigs—these and countless other manifestations of our destructive mania for "growth" are doing irreparable damage to the ocean environment in general and to whale habitats in particular.

About twenty-five years ago, conservationists all over the world began campaigning to change the way humans regard—and treat—whales and their habitats. The result was the massive ecological movement characterized by the slogan "Save the Whales."

4

Save the Whales!

IN THE 1970s, as part of a larger movement to protect the earth's ecology, a huge change came over the way the general public perceived whales and the dangers they face. This change was brought about by a loosely organized grassroots campaign. The whales became the best-known symbol of the environmental movement, and the slogan "Save the Whales" was its centerpiece.

Public awareness

Perhaps the most important aspect of the Save the Whales movement was the major role it played in bringing large-scale commercial whaling to an end. The movement's efforts to stop whaling included raising public awareness of the whales' plight and lobbying for laws designed to protect remaining whale populations.

The Save the Whales movement had many participants. Biologists, cetologists, and other scientists played important early roles, as they voiced their concerns about the fate of the whales. Conservation organizations such as Greenpeace also focused attention on the crisis through their energetic campaigns to halt whale hunting. Meanwhile, politicians and diplomats, the people responsible for passing crucial protective laws, also exerted considerable influence.

New information, as well as the publicity generated by the conservationists, fostered a great deal of sympathy for whales. The whaling industry came to be seen by the general public as brutally cruel, out of date, and thoughtless.

As people became more aware of whales and their perilous lives, the creatures came to be regarded quite differently than in times past. One book in particular, *Mind in the Waters*, became a sort of bible for the movement; its editor, Joan McIntyre, summed up the new attitude by writing that the whale was "on the one hand viewed as product, as resource, as an article, an object to be carved up to satisfy the economic imperative; on the other . . . as the great leviathan, the guardian of the sea's unutterable mysteries."

Members of the Save the Whales movement work on a wooden sculpture of a baby gray whale in a 1977 photo. These activists toured the country to educate Americans about the threat facing whales.

No longer were whales fearsome or distant; now they were increasingly seen as mysterious, fascinating, and gentle giants. They also became important symbols of man's increasing knowledge about the earth's fragile ecology. Scientific breakthroughs helped increase this newfound awareness, a point that writer David Rains Wallace highlights:

> Conservationists and the general public did not pay much attention to Antarctic whale slaughter in its heyday. It took place far from civilization at a time when communication was much slower than it is today. Moreover, people knew much less about the whales' fascinating qualities; science had yet to discover many of them. According to popular perception, cetaceans were either rather dull or rather dangerous creatures. . . . This perception has changed radically in the past three decades, largely because knowledge has increased and communication is better.

New discoveries

Until the 1970s, biologists who studied whales knew surprisingly little about their subjects. Certain aspects of whales' lives—especially the whales that swim in the deepest part of the ocean—are still very much a mystery.

Even the most knowledgeable scientists could not provide very satisfactory answers to some of the most basic questions: How do whales breed? What do they eat? How do they survive? Why do they migrate in particular patterns? Why have they evolved in certain ways? As nature writer Barry Lopez comments regarding an especially puzzling species of whale, "We know more about the rings of Saturn than we know about the narwhal."

Part of the problem has been the difficulty of accurately studying whales over long periods of time. Dissection of a dead animal can reveal a great deal about anatomy, but it is no substitute for observing a living creature. Yet keeping whales in captivity is impractical and, in the opinion of many, a needless form of cruelty.

Only one great whale has ever been maintained in captivity: Gigi, a Pacific gray whale, was captured in infancy in 1971 and spent eight months at Sea World in San

Keeping whales in captivity has drawn criticism from those who regard it as a needless form of cruelty. Other people believe it is necessary for research purposes and to help focus public attention on whales.

Diego, California, before being released. Smaller whales, such as orcas and belugas, are tourist attractions and study subjects at a number of aquariums around the world, but this captivity is a source of controversy. As cetologist Nigel Bonner writes:

> Many individuals and some wildlife societies are strongly opposed to taking animals whose natural habitat is the sea, and confining them in pools which, however large by human standards, must still be tiny in the scale of the ocean. There is a good deal of evidence that many [cetaceans] suffer extreme stress, which may prove fatal . . . even when all reasonable precautions are taken to avoid this.

The best place for a scientist to study an animal is in its natural habitat. Studying whales in their normal

Demonstrators outside of the Japanese Consulate in Seattle protest the capture of five whales in Japanese waters in 1997.

environment, however, used to be a frustratingly slow and inconclusive job. Since whales spend so much time in remote regions, and often avoid ships when they do surface, researchers often had to settle for brief, far-off glimpses of their subjects. However, in the 1970s, new identification techniques and technological breakthroughs revolutionized whale research.

Tracking whales

One of the most important of these advances was a system, developed in the early 1970s, that effectively identifies whales by their markings, which are as distinctive as human fingerprints. Nicks, scratches, and differences in skin coloring make it easy for researchers to distinguish among individuals. By the mid-1970s, hundreds of individual whales had been identified, photographed, and catalogued. This record made it possible to track particular whales and observe how they lived over time, rather than relying on isolated sightings.

Also crucial were new advances in underwater filming. These breakthroughs were important on a scientific level, since they allowed researchers to carefully study films of whales in the wild. But they were also important in raising the public's awareness of the creatures.

One example of the usefulness of innovations in underwater filming is an immensely popular series of television documentaries produced by Jacques-Yves Cousteau. With these shows, Cousteau probably did more than any other individual to advance the cause of the whale, convincing the general public that they were fascinating subjects and worthy of concern. Researcher Cynthia D'Vincent, who specializes in studying humpback whales, writes:

Though we have been working with humpback whales for many years, we never cease to learn new aspects of their complex and subtle behavior, nor does respect and admiration for the wonder of these magnificent creatures ever diminish. Yet there is only so much we can do to save them. Scientists alone do not hold the key to the preservation of the seas and their inhabitants. This will require an awareness on the part of thinking, informed and caring people, in every society that impinges upon the humpback whales, and upon the fragile waters in which they live.

Are whales smart?

Researchers have long been interested in studying the apparently high intelligence of whales. It became clear from studies in the 1970s that whales (as well as dolphins and porpoises, the other animals in the cetacean group) exhibit many traits that experts commonly associate with intelligence. For instance, they are social animals, looking out for one another and communicating with other whales by means of a sophisticated nonverbal language system.

The debate over whether whales are truly intelligent is still going on, but the related research has helped nurture public interest. By letting people know that whales have brains and social interactions that in some ways resemble those of humans, researchers were able to make a once-distant subject seem even more intriguing and relevant.

Some experts, however, are not yet convinced that sophisticated communication and other aspects of whale behavior are signs of intelligence. Ion Lien, an animal behaviorist at Memorial University in Newfoundland, points out that instinct and remarkable adaptations to life in the sea should not be confused with intelligence. As he remarks, "I'm dumbfounded that [whales] can migrate from here to the Caribbean, but it probably doesn't take a lot of what we typically think of as intelligence—creativity and problem solving."

Greenpeace is born

A major element in the movement to save the whales was linked with the explosion of attention to the environment throughout the late 1960s and into the 1970s.

Greenpeace continues its quest to save the whales. Here, members place their inflatable raft in the path of a Japanese whaling ship to protest the killing of whales.

For decades, organizations such as the John Muir Society had advocated the conservation of our waters and wilderness, though this was generally a topic of concern to a relatively small group of people. Then, in the 1960s and 1970s, sparked by such influential books as Rachel Carson's *Silent Spring*, which brought attention to the threat of worldwide pollution, the public gradually realized the importance of environmental protection.

The nineteenth-century term "ecology" was dusted off and applied to new issues in the mid-1970s. The concept fit in perfectly with the mood of the times, which was a period of enormous change around the world on both political and social issues.

Probably the best-known environmental group to come out of the 1970s—and the most prominent in saving the whales—was Greenpeace. Greenpeace began in 1969, when a group of protesters sailed a battered fishing boat into a nuclear test site in Alaskan waters and tried to stop the proceedings. The activists aboard the ship were not able to halt the test, but the event was the first major protest organized by Greenpeace.

Greenpeace expands

Soon, Greenpeace had expanded its concerns to include many other environmental issues, one of which was whaling. Spearheading Greenpeace's assault on this front was Dr. Paul Spong, a psychologist from New Zealand who had done research on communicating with orca whales. Spong and his colleagues organized a bold plan. They decided to directly confront the Soviet whaling fleet in the

Pacific, using small rubber boats to place themselves between the huge whaling ships and their prey.

The Greenpeace activists realized that they could not prevent individual whales from being harpooned. Even assuming that the whalers could be found in the vast seas, the eco-guerrillas, as they called themselves, knew that their boats and equipment were puny compared to the huge, well-organized Soviet fleet. Nor did they think that the whalers would suddenly change their minds when confronted. The Greenpeace strategists knew that they were powerless to immediately stop the slaughter. They suspected, however, that if they filmed the seagoing confrontation and showed it to the world, the results would be dramatic.

They succeeded brilliantly. The films they brought back were highly effective weapons in what became a propaganda war against all the commercial whalers of the world. The moving, highly evocative images—of activists risking their lives in tiny rubber boats to face down gigantic ships, of bloody Soviet whalers slaughtering enormous animals—were seen on television and in publications around the world.

The resulting publicity spurred an explosion of interest in whales. Bumper stickers, posters, and T-shirts with the slogan "Save the Whales" began appearing everywhere. Volunteers collected thousands of signatures on protest petitions to send to the Soviet and Japanese governments, in a move to pinpoint the nations responsible for most of the whaling. A recording of the beautiful, mysterious underwater sounds made by humpback whales, "Songs of the Humpback Whale," became a best-seller.

Whalemania

"Save the Whales" bumper stickers were examples of fads that faded fairly quickly; but the impact of "whalemania" on the public's opinion of whales and whaling was lasting. And this opinion helped sway the actions of politicians and diplomats around the world.

Established wildlife and conservation organizations, such as the National Wildlife Federation, the Sierra Club, the Humane Society, and the National Audubon Society, threw their support behind Greenpeace. Still other groups were organized with the sole purpose of saving the whales; among these were the American Cetacean Society, the Whale Center in the San Francisco Bay area, and the Connecticut Cetacean Society. Hundreds of articles and editorials condemning Japanese and Soviet whalers appeared in scores of newspapers and magazines.

The scruffy little band of Greenpeace activists and their colleagues had started something big. The movement eventually played a major part in creating an international ban on whaling. Some environmentalists saw the movement as a milestone in man's relationship with the environment. As Greenpeace's first president, Robert Hunter, recalls in his history of the organization, *Warriors of the Rainbow*:

> In centuries to come, I was absolutely certain, people would look back on these recordings of ours—the films and tapes and notebooks, the charts and the readings [of the encounters at sea]—and say "Look, here, this is where the turning point occurred. . . . It was the real beginning of the brotherhood between living creatures."

The U. S. government takes action

As the grassroots movement to save the whales gathered momentum, it affected political and diplomatic actions. The United States was the first country to pass protective laws of its own and to take a public stand in favor of the whales in international regulatory agencies. In part, this was because America no longer had an economic interest in whaling; its fleet had gradually dwindled, and the last American commercial whaling station closed in 1972.

The major victories for conservationists in the United States were two laws that went into effect in the early 1970s. In 1972 Congress passed the Marine Mammal Protection Act (MMPA). This law bans the killing by Americans of all marine mammals (including whales), as well as the importation into the country of marine mammals or any products made from them.

The following year saw the passage of an even broader law, the U.S. Endangered Species Act (ESA). This crucial law gives special protection to many animals that are on the verge of extinction. It does this in several ways, such as restricting commercial hunting and protecting critical wildlife habitats. Despite the almost total absence of commercial whaling in U.S. waters, the ESA was a very important weapon in the struggle for the conservation of the creatures. The species listed as endangered were the blue, bowhead, fin, gray, humpback, right, sei, and sperm whales. Since the passage of the bill, gray whales have been removed from the list.

Other laws gave limited power to America in protecting whales from the fleets of other nations. One gave the president authority to impose economic sanctions against countries that violated IWC regulations. Another extended exclusive fishing rights for U.S. ships from twelve miles

© Padry/Rothco. Reprinted with permission.

to two hundred miles from its shores. This law was not designed specifically for the protection of whales, but (since marine mammals are protected within U.S. waters) it effectively does protect whale species that live close to American shores.

The international ban on whaling

Internationally, the move toward conservation of endangered species was slower. In 1976 an international law designed along the lines of the ESA came into force. It is called the Convention on International Trade in Endangered Species (CITES) of Wild Fauna [animals] and Flora [plants]. The bill sets up a legal framework for the full protection from hunting and trade of several species of endangered animals, including gray, right, humpback, and blue whales, as well as to specific populations of fin and sei whales (but not all fins and seis).

By 1978, however, only forty-six countries had agreed to sign the convention. Some of the major whaling nations, including Japan and Norway, were among the countries that refused to sign.

The IWC continued to reject all calls for a whaling ban, meanwhile, though it did begin reducing catch quotas for the commercial whalers under its jurisdiction. Then, in 1979, the commission bowed to international pressure to slow whaling. It declared the Indian Ocean a sanctuary for cetaceans—that is, a designated area in which these species can live without being hunted by commercial whalers. In 1994 the IWC voted (with only Japan opposed) to establish an even larger sanctuary, 11 million square miles wide, in the Antarctic. This move was important because the South Polar region is the primary feeding ground for several species of great whales. This sanctuary will be in effect at least until the situation is reviewed in 2003.

In the period between 1979 and 1994, the IWC made slow changes in its operations. The organization expanded its membership and opened its sessions to outside observers and the media. This new practice lets the public

see the political and economic forces that dominated what many felt should have been an area of humanitarian concern. Whale expert Richard Ellis summarizes popular feeling: "The world wanted to know who was killing the whales, and who was allowing it to happen."

Meanwhile, in 1982, the IWC approved the law that environmentalists had championed for over a decade. It banned all commercial whaling, worldwide, for an indefinite period starting in 1986.

Japan, Norway, the USSR, Brazil, Iceland, South Korea, and Peru—the only countries that still had large commercial whaling operations—opposed the ban. All these countries continued their whaling in spite of international protests. The IWC had no power to act against violations, except by issuing verbal protests.

Even today, a few countries continue to hunt whales despite the moratorium; the ban has not been completely

A Japanese ship sits at Nagasaki port after returning from a whaling expedition. Japan contends that whaling is necessary for research purposes.

effective. Japan and Norway, the countries primarily responsible for the continued whaling, contend that the practice is necessary for research purposes, although the meat is sold commercially.

In 1992 Norway announced that, according to its research, minke whales were no longer in danger. The nation decided therefore that it would resume catching minke whales for oil and meat. Norwegians, they argued, have always hunted minke whales, as they have always hunted elk and reindeer. Norwegian whalers killed 226 minkes the following year.

Although many experts disagree, the Norwegian government continues to contend that the species is in no danger of extinction. Norway's prime minister, Gro Harlem Brundtland, says, "We cannot allow uninformed sentiment to decide on the controlled use of our natural resources." Georg Blikfeldt, a lobbyist for the Norwegian whaling industry, adds,

> Nobody wants to hunt the large whales any more because they are threatened. But the argument that whales must therefore not be hunted at all is like saying that because one breed of pig is on the verge of dying out, nobody should eat pork.

Saving the whales one by one

Much of the debate and action about saving the whales has taken place on a global scale, involving years of discussion, enormously complex laws, and millions of dollars. Yet a different, much smaller method of saving the whales exists as well; it is seen when people band together, sometimes across national borders, to save individual whales.

In a sense, rescuing a single whale is not as important as ensuring the survival of the species as a whole. But keeping the world's attention focused on whales as individuals—as animals that live, breathe, bleed, and deserve concern—is extremely important to the environmental cause.

One such rescue occurred in the spring of 1981, when a young, seriously ill sperm whale became beached at Coney Island in New York City. Rescuers towed Physty (as he was called, after his scientific name, *Physeter*) to an

empty marina, where cetologists and volunteers administered medicine to cure his pneumonia. After a week the whale was swimming strongly and was guided out to sea. By this time, Physty had been seen by millions of people worldwide via news media. The occasion marked the first time a large whale had been successfully rescued and returned to the sea.

In another well-publicized instance, in 1985, a humpback took a wrong turn, swam into San Francisco Bay, and headed up the Sacramento River instead of out to sea. Many techniques were tried to get Humphrey, as he was nicknamed, to reverse his course. Cetologists broadcast killer whale sounds, spectators played flutes and tambourines, psychics sent him telepathic messages, and the military buzzed him with helicopters. Unmoved,

Marine biologists attempt to keep Humphrey the humpback whale wet as a Coast Guard boat approaches. Humphrey made international news in 1985 when he swam off course and ended up in the Sacramento River instead of in the ocean.

Humphrey continued up the river for seventy miles before finally turning around and swimming out to sea.

As with Physty, the event made international news; Patricia Warhol, the executive director of the American Cetacean Society, later wrote, "Surely no whale—possibly excepting the one alleged to have swallowed Jonah, or Melville's mythical Moby Dick—ever received so much publicity, or inspired so much interest." Until, that is, an even more dramatic event took place three years later.

Operation Breakthrough

In October 1988, three gray whales became trapped in the ice off Point Barrow, Alaska. They were found by an Eskimo whaler, who wanted to butcher them to "put them out of their misery." The Native American knew the whales could not survive on their own. But when the story reached the rest of the world, it inspired a widespread determination to rescue the three prisoners.

A huge campaign to save the three whales suddenly descended on the remote northern community: Operation Breakthrough took three weeks to complete and cost over a million dollars, much of the funds and equipment being provided by the oil industry, which was eager for positive publicity to offset its unpopular drilling activities in the Far North. Finally, after several methods had been tried, two Soviet icebreakers were brought in to cut a path to the open sea.

One of the whales disappeared, probably because it panicked and swam under the ice, but in the end the rescue was generally considered a success. First of all, two of the three whales survived. Also, the project represented an unusual collaboration between two countries that had long been uneasy with each other, as well as a cooperative effort among other groups that often were in conflict: Eskimos, environmentalists, and the oil industry. And heavy media attention—including worldwide TV broadcasts of the operation from beginning to end and a phone call to rescuers from President Ronald Reagan—helped keep the focus on whales in general.

Was it worth it?

Some critics have questioned the enormous expense and attention devoted to rescues such as Operation Breakthrough. After all, the gray whale is not an endangered species, and the predicament of the three trapped whales off Point Barrow was not due to human activities.

Was it a worthwhile investment, critics asked, to put so much time, energy, and money in trying to save three wild animals? Or was it simply an exercise in public relations? Columnist Susan Nightingale of the Anchorage, Alaska, *Daily News* comments:

> On the front page of this newspaper, below the story about the whales, was a report that 5 million American children may suffer from chronic hunger. . . . Yet it is the whales, barnacled and bloody, that haunt, that capture our imagination and our prayers—and no doubt our dollars if we thought they would help.

A volunteer uses an ice chisel to expand a breathing hole for one of the three gray whales that was trapped in the ice off Point Barrow, Alaska, in 1988. Critics of the rescue questioned whether the enormous expense involved in saving these whales was justified.

© Punch/Rothco. Reprinted with permission.

ROTHCO

(C) Punch

"Save the blue whale . . . save the blue whale . . . save the blue whale . . ."

Nightingale goes on to point out that President Reagan, who had seen fit to telephone about a couple of whales, had failed to call when seven Eskimos had died on the ice the preceding June.

Many environmentalists, however, would argue that Operation Breakthrough provided value by allowing the general public to see whales as individual animals, not as abstract numbers or faraway, exotic creatures. Also, environmentalists say, such events are important to international relations.

A great deal has been done, around the world and over the years, to stop the slaughter of whales, to protect them, and to increase public awareness of their plight. The whaling industry has virtually ended, in part because whales were hunted nearly to extinction but also because of the efforts of environmental groups and concerned individuals.

Still, many questions remain about the future of these amazing creatures. Conservationists fear, in particular, that the populations of some species may be too small to permit long-term survival. Whaling still takes place to a limited degree, and other dangers remain. The future of the whale is uncertain.

5

The Future

As far as scientists know, no species of whale has become extinct within the last thousand years, despite the devastation caused by whaling and pollution. In fact, there is some evidence that a few species have begun to come back in larger numbers since measures to protect them were put in place.

However, the future is very uncertain for whales in general. Some species still hover on the verge of extinction. The bowhead may be the most endangered of all the whales, though some experts feel that the right whale is even more endangered. "I doubt if the great whales will ever return in their former numbers," researcher Nigel Bonner writes. "A thoughtful biologist cannot look at the future with much hope."

If whales continue to be protected, it is possible that the birthrate of some species will increase over time until it reaches equilibrium—that is, the point at which the number of births roughly equals the number of deaths. However, this will take a very long time, in some cases, perhaps hundreds of years. Even if a given species does reach equilibrium, the number of animals will be much smaller than the original, prewhaling population. It is possible that most endangered species will never get back to their original numbers, no matter what humans do.

Breeding problems and other obstacles

In addition to the ongoing problem of pollution, several factors will affect the ability of whales to regain their original populations, or even to survive. One is the low reproductive rate of whales; another is their isolation. There are so few whales in the vast oceans, with noise pollution further isolating them by preventing them from communicating, that males and females will have increasing difficulty finding each other in breeding seasons. Also, the supply of food for whales is limited and becoming scarcer all the time, largely as a result of competition from commercial fishing fleets.

Every environment is constantly changing, and perhaps it is the natural order of things that some species of whales should die out. Those who take this view point out that an estimated 99 percent of all species that once lived on earth are now extinct. It is normal, they say, for one species to become extinct and another to take its place. Diane Ackerman, a distinguished natural history writer, points out in her book *The Rarest of the Rare* that nature's constant state of change poses a dilemma for humans who are concerned about the environment:

> Some believe that all life is sacred and therefore all species must be preserved. Others argue that what is sacred is the mechanism of nature, and that one of nature's ways is to abort species that aren't adapting well, and to burn down forests as a means of refertilizing the soil. That makes more resources and space for other species.

In other words, some species of whales will, in the normal course of nature, become extinct because they are unable to adapt to a changing environment. Of course that environment is being shaped more and more by human intervention.

The gray whales return

Gray whales once thrived in the North Atlantic, but that area is now devoid of the great creatures. Another group of grays off the coasts of Japan and Russia has also been virtually exterminated. However, one of the few success stories in whale conservation has been the revival of the California gray whale.

Once hunted widely, these whales have been protected since 1946—when there were probably only a few dozen

individuals left—and have made a remarkable recovery. Current estimates range from 18,000 to 23,000, roughly the same population present before whaling. Statistically, this is a much stronger recovery rate than that for any other species of whale.

The reasons for the rapid recovery of this single species are not clear. Probably its particular feeding habits and its liking of shallow waters have helped, since shallow continental shelves are reliable and fertile grounds for plankton, the tiny plants and animals the gray whale eats. Also, grays seem to be unusually capable of withstanding stresses, such as strandings and the hordes of whale-watching boats that observe them during their migrations. Another element is the failure of any other species to move into the gray whale's feeding grounds, a development that might have prevented its rebound.

The gray whale's recovery rate has been so successful that it is no longer considered endangered. In 1994 it was

A gray whale calf pokes its head out of the ocean water. While the gray whale population has virtually disappeared in some areas, the California gray whale population has increased dramatically since 1946.

Experts believe the right whale might be making a slow comeback. Though the populations are still small, right whales have been seen in increasing numbers.

officially delisted (removed) from the ESA's list of endangered and threatened species. However, every five years, the gray whale's status will be reviewed by the U.S. Fish and Wildlife Service, the agency that maintains the list.

Return of the right whale?

There is some evidence that the right whale population may be slowly increasing. There were probably only a few dozen right whales alive at the turn of the century. Though the species has been protected internationally since the 1930s, experts worried that it would become extinct.

Evidence to the contrary began to mount in the 1950s, when researchers discovered a rare sight—right whales swimming in the Atlantic off the coasts of Florida and Georgia, where they had not been seen for many years. By the 1970s, right whales had also been spotted off Cape Cod and Nova Scotia. The populations are still very small—one recent count reported about 800 individuals in

Massachusetts and about 230 in Florida—but cetologists find the numbers encouraging.

Meanwhile, in South Africa and Australia, where right whales were the first species to be virtually eliminated, female right whales and their calves have been spotted in waters close to shore. However, they have not reappeared in significant numbers in their other traditional waters, off the coasts of Japan, Alaska, and Siberia.

No one knows why right whales are not being seen in larger numbers. After all, they have been protected longer than grays. One theory is that the effects of pollution hit the species especially hard. Right whales in the North Atlantic, for instance, live in a heavily toxic part of the sea. And there is still another possibility: some experts believe the right whale population will never fully recover because sei whales (which are not as endangered) have occupied the ecological niche the right whale once filled, and are now eating its food supply.

The future for blues and humpbacks

The blue whale, the largest creature to inhabit the earth, is still severely endangered. Despite twenty years of protection, the species shows only limited signs of recovery.

It is estimated that over 400,000 blue whales once swam in the world's oceans; at the turn of the century whaling had reduced this number to 5,000. The best estimate of the current population worldwide is about 12,000, according to a study cited by the Associated Press in 1996. The largest single concentration of blue whales is a group of about 2,000 in a marine sanctuary off the Channel Islands of southern California.

The number of humpback whales in the North Pacific was estimated at 15,000 around the turn of the century. By 1966, when the humpback became protected, whaling had reduced this number to about 1,200. The figures have since improved slightly—the present North Pacific total is estimated at 3,000—but the North Pacific humpbacks are still in a precarious position. The same is true for humpbacks in other regions. There are an estimated 2,000 in the

North Atlantic, and only about 2,500 remain of the estimated 100,000 that once thrived in the Southern Hemisphere. Thus the possible worldwide humpback total comes to about 7,500, though some experts think the true number is far lower.

No one knows why the humpback population has failed to recover. One theory is that the humpback's calving grounds, such as those in Hawaii, have been subject to especially intense interaction with humans. Another is simply the time factor: gray whales have had twenty more years to recover than humpbacks have had.

Beginning in the late 1970s, researchers noted reports of humpbacks feeding in new territory, such as the inside waters of the islands off British Columbia. This is an encouraging sign that the species may be starting to thrive. As nature writer Bruce Obee observes, "If gray whales are an example, and if we humans have the sense to keep our

The future looks promising for sperm whales. Due in part to the continuing ban on whale hunting, there are close to 2 million sperm whales in the world today.

oceans intact, there's reason for optimism about the humpback's future throughout the North Pacific."

The future for other endangered whales

There is some evidence that sperm whales are not seriously endangered. It is estimated that there may be as many as 2 million sperm whales in the world today, or about 80 percent of the original stock. But many cetologists are worried about figures indicating that the reproductive rate for these whales is dropping, and they fear that the estimates of current populations are much too high. In the meantime, the ban on hunting sperm whales remains in effect, and any trading in their products is still prohibited.

There were at one time at least 50,000 bowhead whales, and probably many more, in the Arctic Ocean. This population dropped to less than 3,000 when bowhead whaling was at its peak before the turn of the century. However, there is evidence that bowheads are making a slight comeback. Estimates of current stocks suggest a current population of about 3,000 to 4,000.

Fin and sei whale populations worldwide were also severely reduced, perhaps by one-half to two-thirds, by hunting. Today, they show little sign of recovery. Minke whales, among the last species to be actively hunted commercially, continue to be hunted, mostly by Japan and Norway, and the population figures of remaining stocks are fiercely debated. Some conservationists argue that the minke should be officially declared endangered; the Norwegian and Japanese governments insist it is in no danger. However, as researcher Nigel Bonner notes, the argument makes no difference to the whale: "[T]he distinction between a scientific quota and a commercial catch will be obscure to a whale with a harpoon in its back."

Watching the whales

Watching whales in their native environment has become a popular pastime for the general public. Spurred on by an increased awareness of and interest in cetaceans, more and more people turn out every year to watch whales

Tourists in the Pacific Northwest view a pod of orcas as the whales make their annual migration into the area.

in action. The popularity of whale watching may have a major effect—both positive and negative—on the future of all whales.

Most of the spectator activity is concentrated on the gray whales that migrate along the Pacific coast. It has been estimated that a million visitors a year gather just at one spot—Point Loma above San Diego Bay—to watch the gray whales pass by on their annual journey. But observers can also have close interactions with humpbacks in Alaska and Hawaii, with beluga whales in Alaska and the St. Lawrence estuary, and with orca and gray whales in the Pacific Northwest. More ambitious "nature safaris" to far-off locations, like breeding lagoons in South America, are also becoming popular.

Sometimes people simply watch from the land, although many prefer expeditions on the water. Typically, a small launch takes watchers a short distance out to sea, close enough to view the whales but not close enough to violate federal laws against harassment. Gray whales seem to enjoy interactions with boats that are not threatening them, and if watchers are lucky, a whale may swim thrillingly close to their vessel. According to nature writer Bruce Obee:

> Many [gray] whales of both sexes and all ages have become friendly. Sometimes they seem to attract one another, gathering in groups. . . . The growing number of friendlies suggests the animals are becoming accustomed to whale-watchers. Mothers who freely allow their calves to interact with people must not see humans as a threat.

Does whale watching create dangers?

The popularity of whale watching pleases most experts who are concerned with conservation, though they point out that the activity's popularity could lead to problems in the future. In the short term, whales generally do not seem to mind boats that keep their distance. One research study in Baja California concluded that the limited amount of whale watching there had no negative effect on the animals. The whales did not shift away from their lagoons

Weary passengers wait patiently in hopes of catching a glimpse of a passing whale. Currently, whale watching does not seem to pose much of a threat to whales, but experts are not certain what long-term effect, if any, whales will suffer from the encroachment on their habitats.

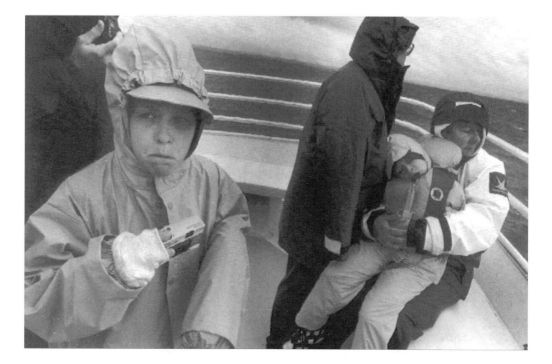

with an increase in tours; in fact, the number of gray whales in the region has risen since whale watching began.

Still, some experts worry that accidents are inevitable, eventually, whenever humans become involved with huge and powerful creatures—even if the creatures are "friendlies." "I think people don't treat them as wild animals," says Dr. Jim Darling, executive director of the West Coast Whale Research Foundation. "There's this image of the whale as something that is not the same as a wild bear, or any other wild animal, [but] it would be better if people were perhaps just a little bit wary."

Further research may also reveal that whale watching has a negative effect on the whales over the long run. Researchers still do not know, for instance, how whales will handle the stress of being approached in their habitats, year in and year out, by speedboats, fixed-wing aircraft, and helicopters.

It will be ironic if on-site observations by the people who most want to help whales end up doing harm to the creatures being watched. But the majority of conservationists and others concerned with whales feel that overall the phenomenon is positive.

An economic alternative

For one thing, whale watching may develop into an important economic alternative to commercial whaling. Spokesmen for the whaling industry often point out that whaling creates jobs. As time goes on, however, seagoing people trained as whalers may find employment operating tour boats and showing off their former prey. Lord Strathclyde, a British environment minister and representative to the IWC, believes the whale watching "may be worth more [financially] than whale-catching."

Perhaps a more important reason given in support of whale watching, however, is that it is another way to educate the general public about whales and the environmental dangers they face. Roger Payne, the scientist who first identified and recorded the songs of the humpback whale, feels that whale watching is an excellent way of arousing interest in the animals he studies and loves. As he tells an interviewer:

> My feeling is *anything* beats extinction. *Anything*! . . . [Some people] say, "Stay away from whales, don't bother them, it's their world, it's not our world," and so on. It's a wonderful position philosophically, but it doesn't do much for the protection of whales. . . . Look at the alternative [to whale watching]. The alternative is an active whaling industry. . . . In that sense, I think whales are better off than they've ever been.

Curbing future pollution and habitat destruction

Pollution and habitat destruction will continue to be the most serious threats to whales in the years to come. Despite

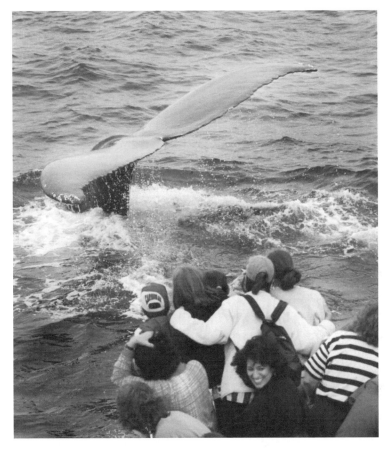

Passengers on a whale-watching boat are treated to the sight of a 35-foot humpback whale raising its tail as it dives in Cape Cod Bay.

the lip service paid to saving the whales, humans are still endangering them by polluting the seas and ruining their habitats. Sometimes this destruction is indirect. For example, researchers in the Pacific Northwest are spending a great deal of energy calculating exactly how much salmon the region's orca population needs to survive. At the same time, however, the salmon's spawning streams—necessary for the survival of the fish, and therefore for the orca as well—are being destroyed by clear-cut logging inland.

Oil pollution will continue to be a major concern as well. Moreover, the full extent of the damage will take many years to assess. By then, researchers fear, it will be too late.

A case in point is the aftermath of the 1989 spill in Alaska's Prince William Sound from the *Exxon Valdez*. The humpback whales that inhabit the sound appear to be there in the same numbers, and their condition appears to

Pollution remains one of the most serious threats to whales today. Here, a cleanup worker walks past the body of a dead beached whale after the 1989 Exxon Valdez *oil spill in Prince William Sound, Alaska.*

be good. However, researchers who conducted an extensive survey after the spill warn in their report that it may be too soon to tell. They point out that it will be many years before a long-lived species like the humpback would be expected to show signs of disease, injury, or reproductive damage that can be blamed with certainty on the crude oil or the chemicals used in its cleanup.

Even if oil companies manage to curb future spills, another area of concern is the habitat destruction created by offshore oil drilling. Noise pollution and other disruptions of the environment caused by drilling on Alaska's North Slope, for instance, threaten one of the last habitats of the bowhead whale.

The ocean, the home of the whales, is the richest ecosystem on earth. However, conservationists say, humans continue to ignore its wonderful variety and precious resources. Instead, through a combination of ignorance and greed, industry uses it as a dumping ground for toxic waste—an action that may have a direct and possibly fatal effect on whales. Charles Mayo, of the Center for Coastal Studies in Provincetown, Massachusetts, had this to say in a speech to the American Cetacean Society in 1990:

> Clearly there can be no hope for the ocean or for its great whales . . . if we do not learn about the ocean what we are coming to realize too late about the land: that toxic wastes come back to poison us from the places where we dispose of them, that their destructive power is too great to be managed, and that their noxious and far-reaching influence lasts longer than we ever thought.

The future of research

In the last few decades, scientists have come a long way in the study of whales. They have discovered much about cetacean social organization, communication, navigation, and migration. However, a great deal remains unknown. Researchers know only a frustratingly small amount, for instance, about breeding, genetics, physiology, and the roles of the senses in the life of whales.

A beluga whale and her calf swim together at a Vancouver aquarium. Although keeping whales in captivity may cause stress on the animals, many experts believe it is still a successful way to keep the public educated about whales.

The main barrier to the detailed study of whales—that they are difficult and expensive to observe—will not come down soon, if ever. The future will no doubt see a continued trend toward studies in the whales' native habitat, with increasingly sophisticated equipment. For example, researchers anticipate technological improvements in such instruments as radio transmitters, photo identification devices, and high-resolution photography that will permit them to track whales from space, via satellite.

Another future trend will be the growing recognition, by scientists and the general public alike, that observing whales in the wild is superior to observing them in captivity. The live capture of smaller whales such as orcas and belugas for use in aquariums is legal today, but this may change in the next few decades. On the other hand, many experts feel that keeping small whales in aquariums, despite the stress it may cause the few animals so confined, will remain valuable for the same reason that whale watching is valuable: because it helps focus public attention on whales.

One controversial aspect of current cetacean research involves the use of dolphins and possibly small whales as military tools. Most of the information on this subject remains top secret, but it is known that the U.S. Navy has spent large amounts of money, time, and energy on cetacean research since the Second World War, much of it apparently focused on training whales to locate objects underwater. In 1987, for instance, the navy confirmed that it had sent a team of dolphins to the Persian Gulf to hunt for mines during the conflict there. This admission unleashed a storm of protest from animal rights activists.

Breeding whales

A less controversial facet of whale research revolves around the possibility of breeding whales in captivity—essentially raising them like cattle in enormous undersea "pastures." Such projects would be similar to the commercial salmon farms that currently exist in many parts of the world.

A conservationist and business consultant, Gifford Pinchot III, was one of the first to study this matter in depth. He proposed creating baleen whale farms sheltered inside coral atolls, tiny doughnut-shaped islands in the South Pacific. Windmills would pump nutrients from the deep ocean outside the atoll to the water on the inside of the "doughnut," fostering the growth of plankton that would serve as food for the whales. The interior of the atoll would thus become a whale breeding ground.

Pinchot proposed this idea in the late 1960s to encourage nations that persisted in whaling for meat and oil to supply themselves with the whales they crave without depleting wild stocks. The slaughter of whales raised in this manner could be controlled and monitored, so deaths and births would take place at the same rate. At the same time, scientists would be able to study the whales at close range.

Whether a migratory creature like a baleen whale would thrive in such an environment, and whether such an enormous undertaking would prove profitable in the end, are only two of the questions that remain open about the idea of farming whales. But some experts say that running a test operation may help ensure the future safety of wild whales.

Finding funding for research

The study of gray whales may also be an important part of future research. After all, the gray whale is the only species that has been resilient enough to make a recovery after coming near to extinction. However, because the grays are no longer hunted or otherwise endangered, government agencies have been reluctant to fund future studies of this species.

A biologist holds equipment used to tag California gray whales. These researchers use a kayak instead of a motorboat as an unobtrusive method of tagging the migrating whales.

Many cetologists are worried about the lack of funding. By learning what has allowed the gray whale to return so strongly, they say, humans would better understand how to help species that have not recovered.

The passionate feelings that sparked the Save the Whales campaign have lessened to a degree, as commercial whaling has largely ceased and laws have been passed to protect the remaining whales. Still, the conservation movement is an important force, at least in Western Europe and North America, and public sensitivity to whales is greater than ever before.

Whales and humans, experts realize, are just two parts of a complex ecosystem. Each small part of this web of life relies on other parts to survive, and upsetting the balance in one place has serious repercussions in others. In his book *The Blue Whale*, George L. Small asks, "When will [man] learn that he is but one form of life among countless thousands, each one of which is in some way related to and dependent on all others? How long can he survive if he does not?"

Because they are protected, some species of whales are actually in less danger of extinction today than are animals of other orders. It is possible that the whales will in time thrive and, indeed, outlast the human race. However, for now their future is uncertain. Many obstacles must be overcome before it can be assured that whales will continue to swim in the sea. In the meantime, the undersea expert Richard Ellis writes, humans are lucky that whales still exist:

> We must consider ourselves fortunate that enough of the great whales escaped the harpoon to enable us to sense the majesty of these creatures. . . . Singing humpbacks, hundred-foot blues, mass-migrating grays: surely they represent a most moving and significant aspect of our natural heritage. Without them we would be diminished by an emotional factor far greater than the tremendous bulk of the whales themselves.

Glossary

---

ambergris: (pronounced amber-gree or amber-grease) A waxy, grayish substance found in the intestines of sperm whales; valuable because it is used in perfume.

baleen: The fibrous plates attached to the upper jaw of a whale of the suborder Mysticeti, enabling the animal to filter krill and plankton from the water for food. Whales of this suborder are called baleen whales.

blowhole: A nostril or pair of nostrils situated on the top of a whale's head, through which the animal breathes.

blubber: The thick layer of fat that protects whales from the cold.

Cetacea: The order of marine mammals that includes whales, dolphins, and porpoises.

echolocation: The system by which an animal navigates using reflected sound waves.

flense: The process of cutting away blubber or skin from a whale.

flippers: The pectoral paddles, or forelimbs, of a whale or other marine mammal.

flukes: The twin lobes of a whale's tail fin.

food chain: The system in which small organisms are eaten by larger ones, which in turn are consumed by even larger organisms.

mammal: A warm-blooded, vertebrate (backboned) animal that produces live young and feeds them milk. Most mammals have hair or fur; in whales, instead, blubber serves as protection from the cold.

moratorium: A ban that legally prohibits an action. Whales are protected by a moratorium that outlaws whale hunting.

myoglobin: An iron-based protein, similar to hemoglobin, that is found in muscle tissue. It helps whales retain large amounts of oxygen while diving.

Mysticeti: The suborder of Cetacea comprising the baleen or whalebone whales. The name literally translates as "mustache whales."

Odontoceti: The suborder of Cetacea comprising toothed whales. The name literally translates as "toothed whales."

order: A taxonomic group of related organisms that ranks between a family and a class, and above a species.

parasites: Plants or animals that live on or in another organism, deriving sustenance or shelter without benefiting the host organism. Parasites often harm their hosts over a period of time.

pelagic: Refers to the deepest part of the open sea. Pelagic whaling involves hunting whale species that range far into the ocean.

plankton: Microscopic plant and/or animal life that drifts passively in the upper layers of the ocean. Baleen whales eat plankton as their primary food.

rorqual: Any baleen whale with numerous pleats or grooves on its throat and belly. The name comes from a Norwegian word meaning "grooved."

scrimshaw: The decorative art of carving on shells, bone, ivory, or, in the case of whales, teeth. Also, items so made.

At one time the work of sailors, who used it to pass the time on long trips.

species: A category of a taxonomic classification. A genus is subdivided into species, and each species defines a group of animals that breed with others in the same species.

spermaceti oil: A white, waxy substance taken from the pool of oil in the head of a sperm whale. It was highly prized as the purest of all whale oils and was often used to manufacture cosmetics, ointments, and candles.

stranding: A phenomenon in which a whale lies helpless on a beach or reef, unable to reach open sea. Unless helped by humans, a beached whale will almost always die. The causes of stranding are unknown.

taxonomy: A system of identifying animals by arranging them in groups based on common characteristics.

whalebone: *See* baleen.

Organizations to Contact

Greenpeace
1611 Connecticut Ave. NW
Washington, DC 20009

One of the most prominent organizations concerned with the environment, and the primary sponsor of the Save the Whales movement. Greenpeace has many local branches in addition to its headquarters in the capital.

Marine Mammal Stranding Center
PO Box 773
Brigantine, NJ 08203

A research and information facility that focuses on helping sea mammals, including whales, that have become stranded on beaches.

Okeanos Ocean Research Foundation
216 E. Montauk Highway
PO Box 776
Hampton Bays, NY 11946

Provides the public with information on new forms of ocean research.

Scripps Institution of Oceanography
University of California at San Diego
A-033B
La Jolla, CA 92093

One of the most distinguished centers for ocean research. Provides information to the public as well as conducting research.

Friends of Long Marine Laboratory
c/o Institute of Marine Sciences
University of California at Santa Cruz
Santa Cruz, CA 95064

Support group dedicated to providing public information and support for various aspects of oceanography.

The Whale Museum
PO Box 945
Friday Harbor, WA 98250-0945

Provides public information and exhibits about whales, especially gray whales and orca whales. Also conducts research on orcas.

The Whaling Museum
Box 25
Cold Spring Harbor, New York 11724

Has exhibits (and some information by mail) about whaling and whales, from past times to present.

Suggestions for Further Reading

Herbert Buchsbaum, "The Fight of Their Lives," *Scholastic Update*, April 16, 1993. A brief article about the plight of endangered whales.

Robert Gardner, *The Whale Watchers' Guide*. New York: Julian Messner/Simon & Schuster, 1984. A good basic introduction to whales in general.

Ada Graham and Frank Graham, *Whale Watch: An Audubon Reader*. New York: Delacorte, 1978. Somewhat dated, but clearly written and still useful as a resource guide. Written in conjunction with the Audubon Society, one of the oldest and most important nature conservation groups.

Patricia Lauber, *Great Whales: The Gentle Giants*. New York: Henry Holt, 1991. A clearly written introduction and overview, specifically for young adults, that focuses on the great whales.

Kenneth Mallory and Andrea Conley, *Rescue of the Stranded Whales*. New York: Simon & Schuster, 1989. An interesting recounting of how three whales beached in New England were rescued and returned to the sea in the winter of 1986–1987.

Vassili Papastovrou, *Whale*. New York: Knopf, 1993. A well-illustrated book filled with short informational pieces about whales and a variety of other marine mammals. Not an in-depth study, however.

Steve Parker, *Whales and Dolphins*. San Francisco: Sierra Club Books for Children, 1994. An excellent introductory book, probably the best general book on the subject for young adults. The Sierra Club is one of the oldest and most respected nature conservation groups.

Kara Zahn, *Whales*. New York: Gallery Books, 1988. A large-format book with beautiful photos and clear, informative text. Not specifically written for young adults, but the photos are an excellent place to begin an appreciation for whales.

Works Consulted

Diane Ackerman, *The Rarest of the Rare*. New York: Random House, 1995. Intelligent, complex, and beautifully written essays on endangered species by one of America's best natural history writers.

Associated Press, "Researchers Track Blue Whales Thriving off California Coast," *Seattle Times*, July 22, 1996. A newspaper article about the mysterious resurgence of blue whales along the southern California coast.

Nigel Bonner, *Whales of the World*. New York: Facts On File, 1989. An excellent reference book by a distinguished British expert on marine mammals. Fairly technical, but with good solid information.

Howard W. Braham, ed., "The Status of Endangered Whales," National Marine Fisheries Service, 1984. A special edition of the quarterly journal *Marine Fisheries Review*; somewhat dated, but still a standard reference tool used by marine biologists concerned with endangered whales.

R. L. Brownell Jr., "Status of Whales, Dolphins, and Porpoises Around the World and Their Future," International Marine Biological Research Institute, Kamogawa, Japan, 1989. A highly technical paper on specific populations of cetaceans prepared by an American researcher for a Japan-based research institute.

Joan Burton, *Mind in the Waters*. New York: Scribner's, 1974. A wide-ranging collection of fiction, poems, illustrations, and nonfiction in celebration of the whale. This book, which was extremely influential in the early days of the Save the Whales movement, is dated now but still interesting.

Jeremy Cherfas, "Whaling Ban Stays in Place—For Now," *New Scientist*, May 22, 1993. A British journalist discusses the current state of the international moratorium on whaling.

Jacques-Yves Cousteau and Yves Paccalet, *Whales*. New York: Abrams, 1986. A lavishly illustrated book with an impassioned message. Cousteau is the world's most famous expert on the sea and a leading voice in the movement to save the whales. Some of the information is dated, but the basic message rings loud and clear.

Tim Dietz, *Whales and Man*. Dublin, NH: Yankee Books, 1987. An interesting, if somewhat dry, book about contact with whales by various humans, including researchers, photographers, and whalers.

Cynthia D'Vincent, *Voyaging with the Whales*. Toronto: Oakwell Boulton, 1989. A large book about humpbacks, written by a whale researcher. Limited insofar as it discusses only one species but interesting nonetheless, and enhanced by beautiful photos.

Richard Ellis, *The Book of Whales*. New York: Knopf, 1980. An excellent introduction to the various species of whales, profusely illustrated by the author. Ellis is a leading writer, artist, and expert on marine life, especially whales.

——, "How Much Longer?" *Audubon*, March/April 1994. A brief article by the distinguished marine artist and author of *The Book of Whales*. In the article, Ellis discusses violations of the IWC moratorium and the commission's slow response to such offenses.

——, *Men and Whales*. New York: Knopf, 1991. Essentially an update and expansion of Ellis's *The Book of Whales*, this well-researched, deeply thoughtful, and very insightful book focuses on the history of whaling. Perhaps the most complete book ever written on the relationship between humans and whales, and about the possibilities for the future.

Peter G. H. Evans, *The Natural History of Whales and Dolphins*. New York: Facts On File, 1987. Dryly written, but full of useful basic information on cetaceans in general. The author is a prominent British research scientist.

Douglas Hand, *Gone Whaling*. New York: Simon & Schuster, 1994. An account of a personal search for orca whales in the Pacific Northwest. The author, a writer for the United Nations, sometimes seems more concerned with telling about himself than about orcas, but provides some worthwhile passages.

Robert Hunter, *Warriors of the Rainbow*. New York: Holt, Rinehart, 1979. An entertaining account of the first years of the environmental group Greenpeace, written by its first president.

Matthew Jaffe, "Thar They Blow . . . Again; Gray Whales Make a Grand Pacific Comeback," *Sunset*, November 1993. A magazine article about the return of the gray whale to the Pacific coastline.

Stephen Leatherwood and Randall R. Reeves, *The Sierra Club Handbook of Whales and Dolphins*. San Francisco: Sierra Club Books, 1983. An excellent, comprehensive overview.

Michael D. Lemonick, "The Hunt, the Furor," *Time*, August 2, 1993. A discussion of the plight of endangered whales worldwide.

Anthony R. Martin, *Whales and Dolphins*. London: Salamander Books, 1990. A large, well-illustrated book by a British researcher. The text is not outstandingly informative, but the photos are worth seeing.

Glenn Martin, "Deep Trouble," *Discover*, January 1993. A magazine piece focusing on the effects of pollution on whales.

National Oceanographic and Atmospheric Administration, Annual Report. Silver Spring, MD: U.S. Department of Commerce, 1994. A technical report on the current status of whales and other sea creatures by one of the leading federal agencies involved in protecting the marine environment.

——, *Our Living Oceans*. Silver Spring, MD: U.S. Department of Commerce, 1993. Another book produced by the federal government's oceanographic research arm. The writing is very dry and at times extremely technical, but the book is useful as a source of information.

Bruce Obee and Graeme Ellis, *Guardians of the Whales*. Seattle: Alaska Northwest Books, 1992. A book that focuses on biologists and researchers who specialize in observing whales in their natural environments. Entertainingly written by natural history writer Obee and illustrated with fine photographs by Ellis. Both authors are based in British Columbia.

William F. Perrin, "Why Are There So Many Kinds of Whales and Dolphins?" *BioDiversity*, July/August 1991. An extremely technical discussion of how and why whales have evolved in such varied forms.

Mari Skare, "Whaling," *Environment*, September 1994. A magazine piece that explores the current state of the small but still somewhat active whaling industry.

George L. Small, *The Blue Whale*. New York: Columbia University Press, 1971. An eloquent examination of the largest creature to ever inhabit the earth. Dated, but interesting nonetheless.

Frank Stewart, ed., *The Presence of Whales*. Seattle: Alaska Northwest Books, 1995. A fascinating collection of essays by a wide variety of distinguished nature writers, such as Diane Ackerman, and research scientists, such as Roger Payne, the man who discovered that humpback whales sing.

Harry Thurston, "Poisoned Seas—the Cause of Whale Strandings?" *Canadian Geographic*, January/February 1995. A magazine piece about the effects of pollution as a possible cause of whale stranding.

Tony Wesolowsky, "The KGB's Sea of Slaughter," *E Magazine*, July/August 1995. A brief magazine piece that focuses on how Soviet whalers apparently continued to conduct operations in defiance of the international moratorium on whaling.

Danny Westneat, "Makahs' Request for Whale Hunt Withdrawn," *Seattle Times*, June 27, 1996. A newspaper report on the controversy over the request made by members of the Makah Indian tribe in Washington State to resume ritual hunting of gray whales.

Index

About the Author

Adam Woog is the author of many books for adults and teens, on subjects ranging from inventions and museums to Duke Ellington and Elvis Presley. Woog lives in Seattle, Washington, with his wife and young daughter, near the orca whale pods of Puget Sound.

Picture Credits

Cover photo: © F. Stuart Westmorland/Photo Researchers, Inc.

AP/Wide World Photos, 17, 21, 24, 45, 48, 54, 61, 62, 67, 69, 73, 78, 82, 83, 85, 86, 88, 90

Archive Photos, 29, 35, 36, 40, 56

Archive Photos/Nordisk Pressfoto, 43

Corbis-Bettmann, 11

© François Gohier/Photo Researchers, Inc., 20, 77, 80

© Greenpeace/Culley, 64

© Stephen J. Krasemann/Photo Researchers, Inc., 15

Reuters/Corbis-Bettmann, 51

UPI/Corbis-Bettmann, 59, 71